WALL HALL
FROM FARMHOUSE
TO UNIVERSITY

3 Ivy Cottages
Aldenham.

WALL HALL
FROM FARMHOUSE
TO UNIVERSITY

EDITED BY
DAPHNE TILLEY AND JOAN BEAGLE

A COMPILATION OF MATERIAL
FROM THE ARCHIVES
OF THE
WALL HALL OLD STUDENTS' ASSOCIATION
AND OTHER SOURCES

EDUCATION DEPARTMENT
UNIVERSITY OF HERTFORDSHIRE

First published in Great Britain in 2003 by
Education Department
University of Hertfordshire
Watford Campus, Alderham
WD25 8AT

© Copyright Daphne Tilley and Joan Beagle 2003

All rights reserved. No part of this book may be reproduced or utilized in any
form or by any means, electronic or mechanical, including photocopying, recording or by
any information storage and retrieval system, without permission in writing from
University of Hertfordshire Education Department.

British Library Cataloguing-in-Publication-Data.
A catalogue record for this book is available from the British Library.

ISBN 1 898534 74 7

Designed by Geoff Green@Geoff Green Book Design, Cambridge CB4 5RA.
Printed in Great Britain by St Edmundsbury Press, Bury St Edmunds IP33 3TZ

Front Cover
The Main Drive to the Wall Hall Mansion
(the chestnut tree is now no longer standing.)

CONTENTS

Foreword Professor Graham Holderness — vii
Introduction Professor Chris Cook — ix
Note on Complilers — xi
Acknowledgements — xii

1	The Early History of Wall Hall	1
2	The Buildings of Wall Hall	27
3	Discussion Documents – Purchase of Estate	30
4	The Early Years of the College	40
	Miss A. K. Davies's talk with John Newsom	44
	Miss K. Balfern's memories	57
	Tributes to Miss K. Balfern	66
	Tributes to Miss N. Dickinson	70
	Students in 1946 and 1950	80
5	The Principals and Deans of Wall Hall	86
6	The Official Opening of Wall Hall	88
7	The Malaysian Teachers – 1951	91
8	The 10th Anniversary – 1955	97
9	Memories of Wall Hall	103
	Student memories – P. Saunders	109
	Student memories – M. Sullivan; R. Barden	112
	Student memories – no names	116
10	College Expansion in the 1960's	118
11	Foundation Day Celebrations – 1965	122

12	College Productions	126
13	The Mansion and Grounds	129
14	The Visit by Patrick Gordon Walker	133
	Training to Work with Deaf Children	136
15	Courses Running in 1975	136
16	Wall Hall after 40 years	155
17	Interior Photographs of the Mansion	163
18	The 50th Anniversary 1995	166
19	Otterspool	169
20	Wall Hall Association & the Field Group	174
21	The Parish Church at Aldenham	181
22	Country Walks around Wall Hall	186
23	Conclusion	190
	Sources	191

FOREWORD

From September 2003 the Department of Education will be physically and academically at one with the rest of the university. Integrated with a wider academic community, collaboration in teaching and research with colleagues in other disciplines will be much easier. After all 'Education' is what the whole university is about, and in the Department of Education we have a lot to offer to the university as a whole.

But there are inevitably some mixed feelings among Education staff and students about the move to Hatfield. There are many advantages to the collegiate environment, with its 'village' atmosphere. No-one can deny that Wall Hall is a beautiful place, with its mansion and its landscaped grounds. Every visitor I receive asks me if I'm not going to miss the grass, the trees, that woodland quiet of the early morning with the hares starting up in front of your car. And of course I reply, truthfully, that the sun doesn't always shine there; that no amount of elegant parkland can make up for academic buildings that have seen the best of their time; and that Wall Hall on a December evening with the refectory closed is not the most welcoming of places.

But there's something else that belongs to Wall Hall and that will, whatever we say, pull at some of our heart-strings when we leave. It's something to do with 'tradition', and of course the place itself does have a fascinating history. However, the 'tradition' I'm speaking of began in 1945, when Wall Hall was opened as an emergency training college for women teachers. It then became a conventional training college in 1949, part of the Hertfordshire College of Higher Education in 1976, part of Hatfield Polytechnic in 1987, and hence part of the University of Hertfordshire in 1992. For over 50 years, despite significant changes in the educational environment, one common factor has persisted: the training of teachers.

Tradition is not stasis but successfully managed change. The

Education department of today is utterly different from the College of Education of the past: it does different things, works in different environments, is much more diverse in its activities. Above all I think it would be true to say it is very successful in upholding the high academic standards proper to a university, and fulfilling the stiff requirements of a university department in terms of quality, research, recruitment and commercial activity. Education now routinely receives quality ratings of 'good' and 'very good' from OFSTED across all its provision; and in 2001 scored an 'excellent' in the review process of the Quality Assurance Agency for Higher Education, which assesses on a common scale all academic subjects in all universities and HE colleges.

These accolades are awarded to educational provision that is not by any means simple; not purely 'academic'; not sheltered within an ivory tower; not fully controlled by the provider. Our work depends absolutely on partnerships with schools, with colleges, with LEAs, with an ever-widening range of public agencies. Much of this is very different from the old College of Education days. But for all that, we still owe something to Wall Hall, and to the generations of teacher trainers who have preceded us. In this book, one of the former staff says that it had 'a national reputation of quiet renown'. That reputation is transferable. We will take what is best in the Wall Hall tradition, and rekindle it in a new environment. This fascinating compilation will assist in that process.

PROFESSOR GRAHAM HOLDERNESS
Dean of Faculty of Humanities and Education
March 2003

PREFACE

During my time [1994–2000] as Head of the Education Department of the University of Hertfordshire I came across quantities of historical material and resources concerning Wall Hall and its place in the history of teacher training. Much of this material was scattered around the buildings and I was enormously grateful when members of the Wall Hall Association undertook the task of sorting and classifying this material, uniting it with materials of their own. The Association now has a respectably organised archive to hand over to the Hertfordshire County Archive.

The idea of producing this book evolved early in the sorting and classifying process. We felt that it would be appropriate to produce it as a means of commemorating and concluding 58 years of teacher training at Wall Hall. The major part of the work was undertaken by Daphne Tilley and Joan Beagle, with help from other members of the Association. My role has been one of support, advice – helping things to happen – rather than that of editor. As work proceeded it became clear to me that the commitment that lay behind the endeavour highlighted the extraordinary influence of Wall Hall upon the lives and careers of generations of teachers. I felt that the work became a celebration of, and gratitude for, the professional training received at Wall Hall, both in terms of the place and the people. For some the experience seems to have transformed their lives, and few remained unaffected by the surroundings and atmosphere. This is as true of the staff as of the students, even today. I count myself fortunate in having come to work in such a place.

The material in this book is wide-ranging. It does not pretend to be a work of academic or historical analysis. It is rather a compilation of materials drawn from many sources that would appeal to those who have studied or worked at Wall Hall or those with local connections. It covers the fascinating early history of the Wall Hall estate and its surroundings, the influence of prominent owners, its role in World War II, the post-war processes of setting up the College and the activities of the leading figures therein. There are substantial items of personal reminiscence contributed by staff and former students, which vividly portray their lives at Wall Hall and its influence upon them. For my part I was particularly taken with the post-war processes of setting up the College and the activities of the leading figures therein. Others will prefer to learn about the history of the estate or be reminded of their time at Wall Hall. Whatever the outcome we believe it has been a worthwhile endeavour.

In November 2002, I received the sad news of Daphne Tilley's sudden death. I believe that it would be fitting to dedicate this book as a memorial to her in gratitude for her enormous contribution to its realisation.

PROFESSOR CHRIS COOK
Associate Dean, Faculty of Humanities and Education.
March 2003

NOTE ON COMPILERS

DAPHNE TILLEY entered Wall Hall College as a mature student in 1966 and qualified with a Certificate of Education with Distinction in 1968. She taught at St. Peter's C. of E., J.M.I. School, Rickmansworth; was then offered a position as Head of Music at Maple Cross J.M.I. School, Rickmansworth, which she held until applying for the position as Deputy Head at Rickmansworth Park J.M.I. Regretfully she had to retire in 1992 through severe osteo-arthritis. From 1998 to 2002 she was Secretary of the Wall Hall Association.

JOAN BEAGLE was a student at Wall Hall from 1965 to 1968. After obtaining a Certificate of Education, she taught at Woodcroft Infants School, Edgware, Middlesex. She took early retirement in 1988, taking this opportunity to travel far and wide with her husband.

Since 1997 she has been Membership Secretary of the Wall Hall Association.

ACKNOWLEDGEMENTS

We should like to thank particularly: Trevor May (former History Tutor); Hertfordshire Archives and Local Studies; the Vicar of Aldenham Parish Church, Rev. Robert Fletcher; Ms Mary Hood (former Rural Studies Tutor) all of whom gave permission to include documents and photographs; Miss A. K. Davies (third Principal) who made helpful suggestions, enabling many unwanted elements to be relegated to the Archives; Professor Chris Cook, who gave invaluable advice and support in the compilation and production. (He has also made arrangements for the Archive materials, to be placed in the Hertfordshire Archives and Local Studies (HALS) at County Hall, Hertford. SG13 8EJ. This will enable interested parties either to add further material, or to look for themselves at the documents, photographs, newsletters etc. It would be wise to telephone 01438 737333 or Fax: 01992 555113, prior to any visit, to enable relevant boxes to be retrieved). Thanks are also extended to former Staff and Students who kindly sent photographs, documents and written memories of their association with Wall Hall, and to all others who supported our work. Many visits were made to Wall Hall over two years. On each occasion we were extended a warm and friendly welcome. For this we are grateful to the Dean and other academic staff; to Hilary Hubbard (Secretary to the Dean); Maz White (Reception); the Refectory; Security and portering staff.

DAPHNE TILLEY AND JOAN BEAGLE

CHAPTER 1

THE EARLY HISTORY OF WALL HALL

Wall Hall is situated in Hertfordshire where the great belt of chalk that runs in a north-easterly direction from Salisbury Plain meets the clay of the Greater Thames Basin. There are various deposits of sand, gravel and loam, including Puddingstone, which is unique to Hertfordshire.

The River Colne, which drains the greater part of western Hertfordshire, once ran eastwards, but was diverted by one of the glaciers of the Anglian Ice Age into the old river valley of the proto-Thames. Today it meanders southwards through a wide flood plain to join the River Thames near Staines. A little north of Wall Hall the west bank rises steeply, making it unsuitable for cultivation and was probably wooded at all times. Wall Hall, situated at about 250 feet, looks out over the flood plain, the highest point being just over 330 feet at High Cross – where a gallows stood many years ago. (This could be seen from across the river in St. Albans.)

The history of the area must have been influenced by the nearness to the ancient prehistoric Icknield Way and other trackways and to the great Roman road linking London and St. Albans (Verulamium) – Watling Street. These cities, not many miles away, contributed in their turn to the development of Aldenham and the creation of Wall Hall Manor.

Early flint tools and the remains of a Roman kiln have been found nearby but the general assumption is that the area was heavily wooded and little developed until the coming of the Saxons penetrating perhaps along the roads and the river routes such as the Colne. Before the Norman Conquest of 1066, claims to ownership of the land were made and disputed by the great Abbeys of St. Albans and Westminster. Certainly by the later 12th century there was a Manor here. At that time too, the Church was built at Alden-

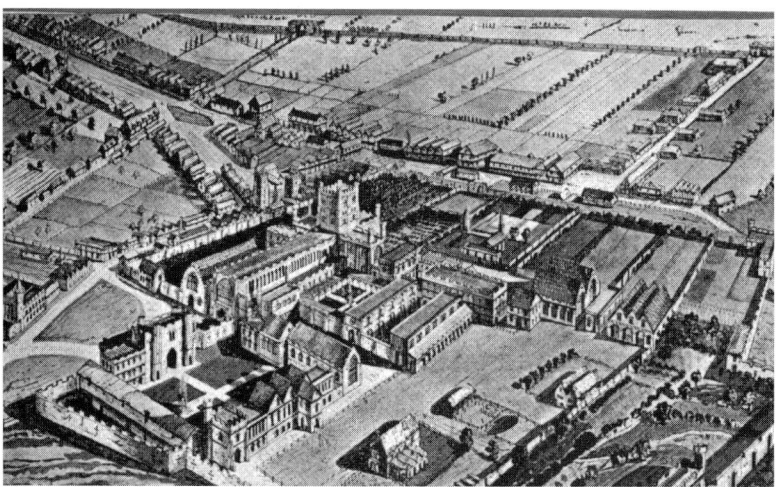

The Benedictine Abbey of St. Albans.

ham, only a small Norman fragment is to be found in the present building.

This small Norman window at the West end of the South Aisle represents St. Augustine of Canterbury – to the memory of Mr Lionel Rickards in 1898 on the 1,300th anniversary of St. Augustine of Kent A.D. 598.

The ownership of both Wall Hall and the Manor of Aldenham nearby, is complicated and obscure. Many names are listed in official records, among them wealthy and influential London merchants who bought land on a considerable scale as a means of investing their wealth and securing revenues. No one family held on to Wall Hall for any length of time. In all probability few, if any, of these owners resided at, or even visited the Manor. We know virtually nothing of who managed the Estate or laboured there. Possibly there was a farm house for the Bailiff or Manager, superior to the dwellings of the peasant labourers. Merchants such as Daniel de Stepney and Guy de Wale Hale were the first to hold the Manor in the late 12th and early 13th centuries. Two women come into the story, Isabella, widow of the Baron Robert de Scales was one. (The Baron had fought with Edward 1 in the Scottish and other wars.) Later, in the 14th century, the Manor was held for a short time by Clementia de Eccleshale.

Monks in Procession carrying the Shrine of St. Alban.

The following extracts illustrate the complexity of the ownership of Wall Hall.

WALL HALL

The earliest reference to WALLHALL (Whalehall), now called ALDENHAM ABBEY, is of about the middle of the thirteenth century, when Guy de Walehale granted to Godwin son of Sampson 'all that land which divides the fees of the abbot of Westminster and the abbot of St. Albans and extends by the way that leads from the court of Walehale towards le Su upon the river and all that land which lies between the said hedge and the land of Christemann in this other side in which land is a well called Fildwell, and extends from the said way upon the said river.'

Godwin granted all the above lands to Saer son of Henry, who had also other land in Wallhall by gift of William son of Adam de Aldenham. And Saer in turn made a grant of land in Wallhall to William son of William.

For about a hundred years after this nothing is known of Wallhall, the next record of it being in 1349, when the so-called manor was the property of Clementia Eccleshall. After her death it was said she had left a will desiring that the estate should be sold and the money from the sale devoted to founding a chantry and paying off debts which her husband Richard had incurred during the time he was treasurer to King Edward III at Calais. Apparently the manor was sold to Geoffery Somery, who re-leased it in 1349 to John son and heir of Richard Somery. Eight years later this John and Margery his wife conveyed the manor to John Golde and William de Farnyngho, chaplains, possibly for purposes of a trust or settlement.

The abbots of Westminster appear to have leased the manor from time to time. In 1361 it was leased to John de Ditton, clerk, with a stipulation that he should not cut the timber, that he should erect a new water mill, and pay the abbot and convent of St. Albans the 4s. yearly which was reserved in the agreement between the two monasteries above mentioned.

At the surrender of Westminster

Aldenham Abbey

Abbey to the crown on 16 January 1539–40, the manor was in lease to Robert Duncombe, and in 1543 the manor court was held in the name of the king. On 1 August 1546, Henry VIII granted it with the rectory and advowson of the church to Ralph Stepneth, and on 12 February 1555, there was confirmed to the said Ralph and Joan his wife, and their men and tenants, freedom from toll for all their goods, as Edward the Confessor had granted to the abbots of Westminster and their men.

The manor and advowson remained in the hands of the Stepneth family, and were sold by Paul Stepneth and Sarah his wife on 20 January 1588–9, to Edward Carey, master and treasurer of Queen Elizabeth's jewels and plate, who was afterwards knighted, and died on 18 July 1617, leaving Henry his son and heir, on whom the manor had been settled at the time of his marriage with Elizabeth Tanfield in 1602. Henry was created Viscount Falkland, and at his death in 1633 he was succeeded by Lucius Carey, Viscount Falkland, his son, who in 1642 sold the manor to Sir Job Harby, bart., a merchant of London. Sir Job died in 1663, and was succeeded by his son Sir Erasmus Harby. The manor was in 1664 sold by Sir Erasmus Harby to Denzil Holles, first Baron Holles of Ifield, from whom it passed to Sir Francis Holles, his son, and then to Denzil Holles, third Baron Holles, who died without issue in 1694, when the manor went to his cousin John Holles, fourth earl of Clare and duke of Newcastle. At the death of the duke of Newcastle in 1711 the manor passed to his nephew, Thomas Pelham, created in 1714 Viscount Pelham and earl of Clare, and in the following year marquis of Clare and duke of Newcastle. He sold it in 1754 to Samuel Vanderwall, a merchant of London, who, at his death without issue, bequeathed it to his stepson Thomas Neate. The manor was sold by Neate in 1799 to George Woodford Thellusson, and was purchased in 1805 by the trustees of his father's will, whereby it went to his brother Peter Isaac Thellusson, created Lord Rendlesham in 1806, in the hands of whose descendant, the present Lord Rendlesham, the manorial rights now are.

The abbot of Westminster claimed the return of all writs in his manor of Aldenham, and many other liberties. There was a custom by which the copyhold tenants elected the reeve of the manor, who collected the lord's rents and delivered to the lord every year two dozen capons, two dozen geese, two dozen hens, and two bushels of oatmeal, for which the lord gave him 22s. and a livery coat, or 10s. instead of the coat.

CASHIO HUNDRED
ST. STEPHEN'S

In 1392 the king made a grant enabling John Mirfelde and John Harpesfelde, probably as trustees, to give this manor with its appurtenances to the prior and convent of St. Bartholomew, Smithfield. The site of the manor and other appurtenances were held of the abbot of St. Albans by knight's service and rent and suit at the hundred court of the abbot at

   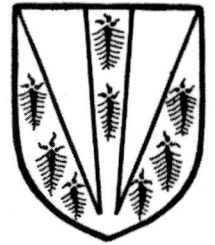

(*left*) Westminster Abbey. **Gules two crossed keys or.**
(*right*) St. Albans Abbey. *Azure a saltire or.*

(*left*) Carey. *Argent a bend sable with three roses argent thereon.*
(*right*) Holles. *Ermine two piles sable.*

Stepneth. *Argent a fesse checky or and gules between three owls azure.*

Pelham, Duke of Newcastle. *Azure three pelicans argent*

Cashio every three weeks, and suit at his court under the ash tree at St. Albans every three weeks. This manor continued in the possession of St. Bartholomew's, Smithfield, until the Dissolution.

In 1544 the king granted this manor to Edward Elryngton and Humphrey Metcalf, who conveyed it in the same year to Sir John Williams, knt., treasurer of the Court of Augmentations, and Christopher Emondes, for the use of the said John. Only nine years later a certain James Jacob laid claim to this property, and stated that Sir John Williams had enfeoffed Richard Bowman, clerk, of the estate, and he in turn had granted it to Jacob. At his death in 1561 James Jacob left the whole estate with frankpledge and court leet to his son Polidore, who alienated it to John Saintsome, yeoman. Saintsome died in 1587, and left the manor to his wife Helen, who survived him three years. The property then appears to have passed to John's son and heir John, who sold it in 1619 to Sir Henry Carey, knt., comptroller of the king's household, Knight of the Bath, Lord-Deputy of Ireland, and in 1620 created Viscount Falkland in the kingdom of Scotland. Seven years before the sale Saintsome had leased the manor to William Ewer of Aldenham for 550 years, and he in 1621 conveyed it to Falkland for the remainder of the lease. Viscount Falkland died in 1633, leaving a son and heir Lucius, and from this date the property descended with the manor of Aldenham (q.v.), until it was sold in 1812 by George Woodford Thellusson to Admiral Sir Charles Morice Pole, K.C.B. He died in 1830, leaving two daughters, to the elder of whom, Henrietta Maria Sarah, wife of

Stuart of Aldenham.
Or a fesse checky argent and azure in a double tressure counterflowered gules.

Henry Cary Viscount Falkland

William Stuart, this property passed under the will of her father. On the death of Mr. Stuart in 1874 it passed to his son Col. William Stuart, who was succeeded in 1893 by his eldest son William Dugald Stuart of Tempsford Hall, co. Bedford, the present owner of the estate.

Aldenham Abbey was in 1899 the residence of Mr Charles Van Raalte, and passed before 1902 into the occupation of Mr John Pierpont Morgan, who now lives there.

Wallhall appears to have ceased to be a manor before 1700 as Chauncy makes no mention of it. Towards the close of the eighteenth century Wallhall was but a farm-house belonging, with lands adjacent, to George Woodford Thellusson, who built the present principal front, about 1800, and called the house Aldenham Abbey. The library, the portico, and the conservatory were added by William Stuart. In the grounds are some spurious ruins made up of fragments from various sources, some of which are said to have come from Aldenham Church.

Extract from *The Victoria County History*, Volume 2, 1908, courtesy of HALS

THE EARLY HISTORY OF WALL HALL

In the late 14th century the Manor of Wall Hall came into the ownership of the London Priory of St. Bartholomew. It would then have been sublet, with the Priory gaining benefit from the revenues. With the dissolution of the monasteries Henry VIII was able to sell and re-assign the ownership of a great quantity of monastic lands. Sir John Williams, a relative of Thomas Cromwell who had ruthlessly carried through the Dissolution Policy, acquired the Manor in 1544. He, as Keeper of the King's Jewel House, had in his care great quantities of confiscated monastic plate.

The Manor continued to pass from family to family often to persons high in royal circles, such as Viscount Falkland who was buried in the village in 1633.

By 1690 the estate had passed to John, Duke of Newcastle, owner of many landed properties.

The more modern history of Wall Hall comes with its acquisition by George Woodford Thellusson who bought it in 1799. He came from a family of originally Huguenot bankers and financiers. His father, Peter Thellusson was responsible for an Act of Parliament in 1800, still in force. This prevented the passing on of money and land to as yet unborn generations. Thellusson in his will had attempted to bypass his immediate descendents, but parliament took the view that such a step could lead, over the years, to an enormous accumulation of capital which might destabilize the Kingdom. The controls of inheritance and income tax were yet to be adopted!

George Thellusson lived at Wall Hall and proceeded to modernize the house in accordance with the taste of the time. He added to the old, simpler house a castellated front; he employed the great Humphrey Repton to landscape the grounds; made new roads and added the still surviving stable clock. The house was renamed Aldenham Abbey in the fashion of the day. On his death in 1811, his widow moved to Otterspool, a house on the Estate.

John, Duke of Newcastle and Clare.
Photograph copied from Hertfordshire Archive & Local Studies.

THE STABLE CLOCK

A familiar feature of the house is the clock on the Stable Block, which was adopted as the College logo. Installed by George William

A map of 1766 – note name of "Wars Hall" on the left, near Otterspool. From the map of Andrew Dury and John Andrews published in 1766.
Copied by permission of the Hertfordshire County Archives.

Thellusson, it was an eight day weight driven pendulum clock, before it was mechanised, with the hours struck on a bell. The frame is of cast iron construction with brass wheels. The timekeeping part has a Graham-type dead beat escarpment and a two seconds pendulum. The name of the maker John Thwaites (of Clerkenwell) is engraved on the end of one barrel, with the date of manufacture, 1801. The original day-books of Thwaites survive in the Guildhall library. They contain the entry for supplying this turret clock and sending a man out to Aldenham to install it. Also

THE EARLY HISTORY OF WALL HALL

Wall Hall c. 1799

Aldenham Abbey, 1860

Members of the Stuart family – mid 19th century.

The Stable Clock

in the day-books is the record of supplying a matching set of 18 inch dial instruments; a barometer; a remote-reading weather-vane and a clock. These instruments would have been in the house, but no longer survive. The most likely site for them is the front hall, or the library next door.

THE ICE HOUSE AT WALL HALL

Many maps show the position of an ice house (which is at the back of the farm buildings.) Ice houses were used as we use refrigerators. They were a luxury only for the wealthy who were able to buy a supply of ice, or have access to a river or lake. Wall Hall was fortunate to be situated by the River Colne. The supply was maintained by storing, in damp sawdust, blocks of ice sawn from the river. The ice house would have been much deeper than this. Over the years it has been filled with leaf litter and branches from the surrounding trees.

NOTES ON THE SUNDIAL AT WALL HALL.

In the times in which we live, it is easy to set our domestic clocks and watches to show the correct time, by means of signals sent by telephone and broadcast by radio. In previous centuries a time

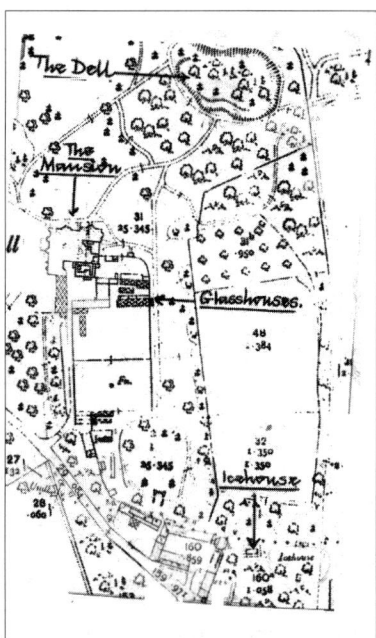

standard had to be established locally by astronomical observation. For precise purposes this was achieved using a transit telescope, but the common method was to use a sundial.

True solar time (indicated by a sundial) and mean solar time shown by a mechanical timekeeper are coincident on only four occasions during the year. In the intervening periods there is a difference of up to about 20 minutes. This difference between true and solar time and mean solar time is expressed as the equation of time and its value must be known to set a clock using a sundial. Tables were published to enable this to be achieved, but the information was also included on some sundials. The sundial was in past centuries a scientific instrument and not merely the garden ornament it is considered today.

The sundial at Wall Hall was mounted on a heavy stone pillar. It is made of brass and is signed, now indistinctly :

G.& C Dolland
Optician to the King
—- Old Bond Street
LONDON

The outer ring is engraved with hours and minutes, each minute

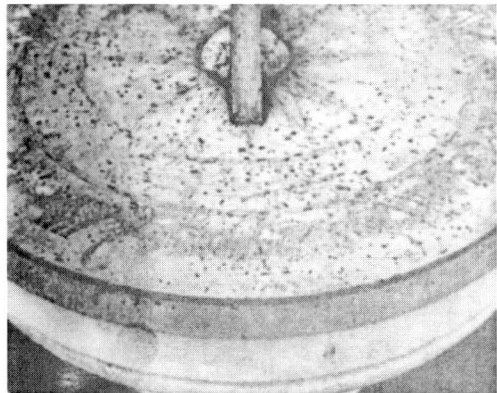

The Wall Hall sundial.

being marked over the maximum range of daylight hours indicated. As usual, the hours are designated with Roman numerals and the minutes with Arabic. On a pair of inner concentric scales the difference between true solar (sundial) and mean solar (clock) time is shown, one of the number of minutes to be added or subtracted according to the day of the month Round the appropriate segments of this scale are engraved "Watch ahead of the sun" and "Watch slow". In the centre of the dial is a compass rose to indicate the correct orientation. 16 points of the compass are shown, each direction being engraved on the innermost concentric ring. It should be noted that the use of the word "watch" in this context does not refer specifically to a timekeeper being carried on the person as it would in present day usage. Literature of about 1800 refers to the watch part of a clock and the striking part of the clock. Thus the watch part was the timekeeping part.

The date of the construction of the sundial is about 1800 and thus contemporary with the turret clock on the Stable Block. It is possible that it was supplied with the clock, but as it is more portable than the clock, the history of the sundial, at the moment is conjectural. However, it does represent a good example of late 18th or early 19th century instrument making, which is not readily apparent under the thick layer of corrosion resulting from centuries to the elements.

[Note: the stone pillar was stolen in 2002; the sundial itself having previously been removed for safe-keeping].

THE EARLY HISTORY OF WALL HALL

Reference

The Mathematical Practitioners of Hanoverian England 1714-1840 E. G. Taylor. OUP 1966.

'Time Measurement'. Part 1. *Historical Review*. F. A. B.Ward. Science Museum. HMSO 1947.

K. J. Ming (a part-time student) October 1980.

THE WELL HEAD

A letter was written to the Victoria and Albert Museum in 2002, asking if the garden ornament, which has been situated outside the old dining room/library/ lecture room at Wall Hall, could be identified.

The reply from Dr. Paul Williamson, Keeper of the Sculpture, Metalworks, ceramics and Glass of the Victoria and Albert Museum states:

> The well head at Wall Hall is almost certainly Venetian and of the late 19th century. Such well heads, in the style of the twelfth and thirteenth centuries, were made in large numbers in Venice and North Italy from about 1850 onwards, to meet the demand of wealthy tourists looking for garden ornaments and were exported throughout Europe and the United States. There are many English gardens – as at Hever in Kent, which were bought by the American William Waldorf Astor – and they regularly come up in auction.
>
> I think it highly likely that the well head was placed at Wall Hall during the occupancy of the Morgans, between 1910 and 1939, as it epitomises their well-educated Italianate taste. Given its connection with the site, rather than the University, it would be appropriate to leave it where it is and hope that the developers would make a feature of it.

Photo by Joan Beagle.

HOUSE SALE

Sir Charles Morice Pole, M.P. bought Wall Hall. He was a distinguished sailor and friend of William IV. He left the Estate in trust to his wife and then his daughter, Henrietta, who had married William Stuart, son of the Archbishop of Armagh. An American connection comes in here, in that his mother was descended from

> **HERTS.**
>
> **The Particulars**
> OF THE VERY
> **ELIGIBLE FREEHOLD ESTATE,**
> PRINCIPAL PART TITHE-FREE,
> **AND LAND-TAX REDEEMED,**
> COMPRISING THE
> *MANOR, or REPUTED MANOR of WALL HALL,*
> LATE THE PROPERTY AND RESIDENCE OF
> George Woodford Thellusson, Esq. M.P. Deceased,
> THE
> **ELEGANT FAMILY MANSION,**
> With Castellated Fronts,
> WELL PLANNED OFFICES OF ALL DESCRIPTIONS,
> BEAUTIFUL PLEASURE GROUNDS, PLANTATIONS, GARDENS,
> FINE STREAM OF WATER,
> Entrance Lodges,
> **FARM, AND LAND,**
> CONTAINING
> **TWO HUNDRED AND THIRTY ACRES,**
> OR THEREABOUTS,
> CALLED
> **WALL HALL,**
> SITUATE IN A FINE HEALTHY AND BEAUTIFUL PART OF THE COUNTY OF HERTS,
> Three Miles from Watford, Five from St. Albans, and Sixteen from London,
> PARTLY SITUATE IN THE PARISHES OF ALDENHAM AND SAINT STEPHEN,
> And partly Extra-Parochial,
> A MOST DESIRABLE PROPERTY FOR A GENTLEMAN,
> And fit for immediate Occupation
> WHICH WILL BE SOLD BY AUCTION,
> **BY MR. ROBINS,**
> At Garraway's Coffee-House, Change-Alley, Cornhill,
> LONDON,
> On THURSDAY, the 28th of MAY, 1812, at TWELVE O'CLOCK, in ONE LOT,

WALL HALL

SALE PARTICULARS – 1812.

1. Wall Hall Mansion, offices, yards, flower garden, kitchen gardens, stables, coach houses etc.
2. Filbert ground, dairy, icehouses etc.
3. Farmhouse, buildings, barns, granary, yards etc.
4. Plantations between the Mansion and Farmhouse.
5. Dell or Grove by Dell Field.
6. Lawn, shrubbery, circular flower garden and pleasure ground.
7. Part of Wall Hall Park, formerly Aldenham Place Farm.
8. Remainder of Wall Hall Park, formerly in Aldenham Place Farm.
9. Part of the Water, formerly in Wall Hall Farm.
10. Remainder of the Water, formerly in Wall Hall Farm.
11. Rough Meadow.
12. Three acre in Legger Shot.
13. Acre piece in Legger Shot and another acre piece in the same, later Cappers.
14. Five Acre Meadow.
15. Six Acre Meadow.
16. Ashey Down.
17. Middle Down.
18. Great Down.
19. Broad Field.
20. Hedge Grove and Plantation in same.
21. Part of Jacketts Lane Field, formerly Hudnutts.
22. Dell Field.
23. Cottage and Garden at Aldenham, in occupation of Dickinson and Pooley.
24. Lodges and Garden at Aldenham, in occupation of Widow Foster and Hawkins.
25. Triangular plantation in the road, by Aldenham Churchyard.
26. Roads and Plantations leading to Wall Hall, formerly in Aldenham Place farm.
27. Bingham Spring, formerly in the same.

(The numbers relate to the positions on the following Map of the Estate.)

THE EARLY HISTORY OF WALL HALL

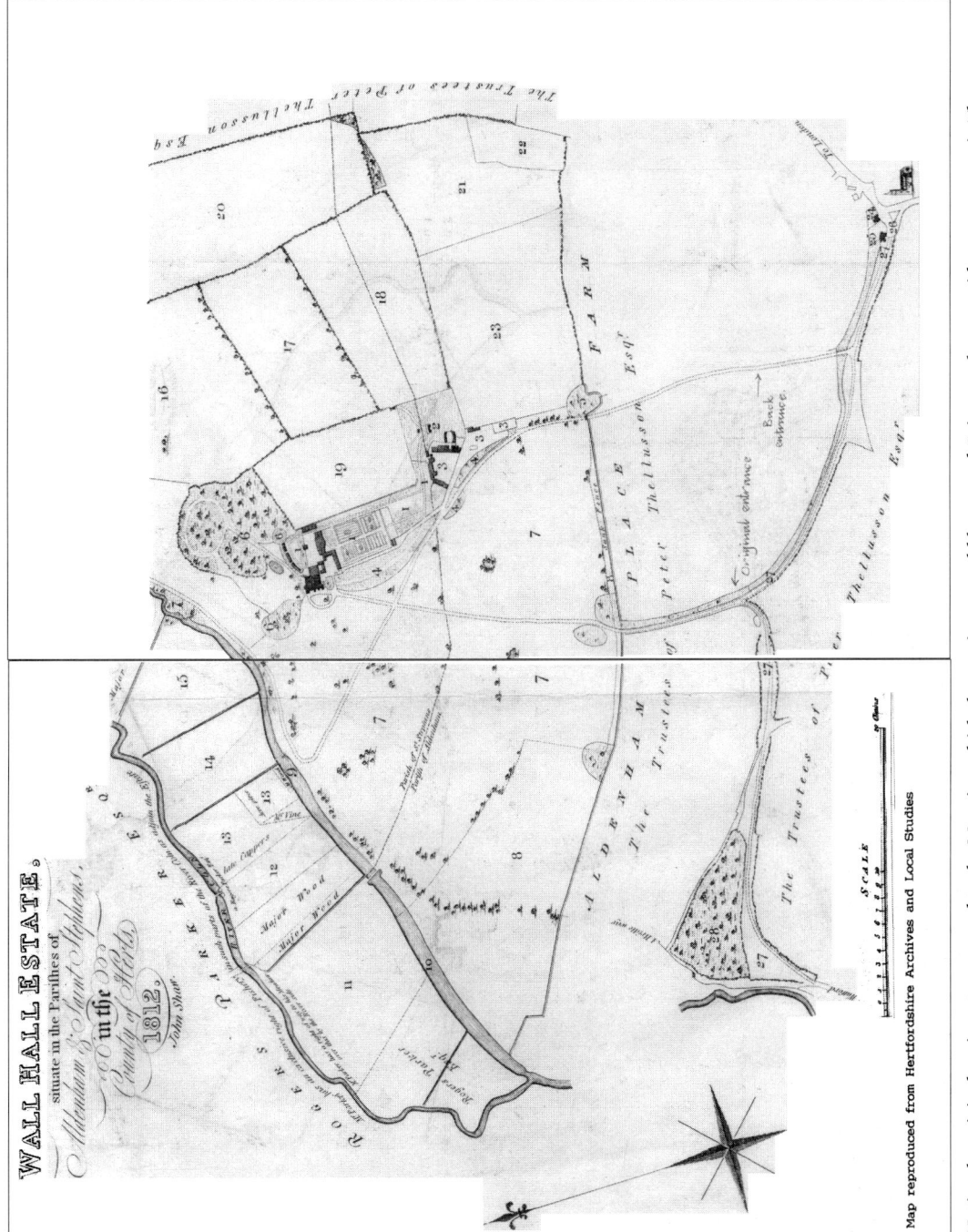

Notice the original main entrance road to the Mansion which the carriages would have used. It is now the one with a gate across it. The present entry road (The Causeway) was the back entrance to the farm and for the servants etc. to use.

William Penn, founder of Pennsylvania. The Stuarts built the four Almshouses in nearby Roundbush.

In 1874, a stockbroker, Charles van Raalte acquired the lease of the house. He added the Porte Cochere, the huge library and a large conservatory (of which one side survives.) On his death in 1808 [1908] the lease passed to an American, John Pierpont Morgan, whose wealth was derived from the building of railways, production of steel and banking. Immensely wealthy, he owned several properties in England and Scotland and like van Raalte, entertained lavishly with Royalty as guests. He spent only a few months of the year at Wall Hall, which he valued for its shooting and for providing fruit, vegetables and flowers for his London residence. He made himself unpopular in the village by closing the pub, of which he disapproved, though he replaced it with a social club. In 1921 he established a flock of Southdown sheep which became of national importance. Morgan was also instrumental in renovating Church Farm and its outbuildings. He appointed a Superintendent, John Fleming, to take over the management and he engaged all the best herdsmen and stockmen to be in charge of the pedigree cattle, Percheron horses, large white pedigree pigs, Southdown sheep and white leghorn poultry. Consequently they won prizes all over Britain and Europe. The dairy shorthorns were housed in what is now the Aldenham Golf Club House.

With the outbreak of war in 1939, Morgan returned to the United States and the Hall was loaned to the American Ambassador, Joseph Kennedy, who stayed there at weekends with his family, including his son John, a future President of the U.S.A. who, when America entered the war arrived at Wall Hall in full naval uniform.

Concern about the sprawling urbanisation had led the Hertfordshire County Council to secure an agreement with Morgan, entitling them to the option to buy the estate when it became available, in order to preserve the open country to the East of Watford. This was before the official Green Belt policy came into force. When Morgan died in 1942 the Council bought the Estate.

In the war years the house served a variety of purposes. At one time it was used for training special agents to work with the Resistance groups in the Low Countries. The old quarry, the Dell, it is said, was used for training in pistol shooting. During the V1

THE EARLY HISTORY OF WALL HALL

(*previous page*) Map reproduced from Hertfordshire Archives and Local Studies.

The Almshouses

Rules and regulations for inmates in the Almshouses.

I.

Each house must be kept in a state of great cleanliness and neatness. The garden allotted thereto must be properly cropped and weeded; and great personal cleanliness must be observed by each inmate.

II.

No inmate is allowed, under any pretence, to take in a lodger; nor is any member even of their own family allowed to dwell with them. But in case of sickness, a nurse will be permitted, if necessary, but subject to the approval of WILLIAM STUART, ESQ., or the Patron of the Charity for the time being.

III.

That the Inmates shall on all occasions be willing and ready to assist each other, both in sickness and in health; and endeavour, by every means to live in perfect love and harmony together.

IV.

It is expected that each Inmate will be regular in attendance on Public Divine Service, and not neglect to partake of the Holy Communion, whenever it is possible; and that they all will strive to let their general behaviour be such as becomes Christians.

V.

All immorality, of whatever kind, and in particular Drunkenness, Swearing, or using any bad language will be punished at the discretion of the Patron.

VI.

In addition to the annual gift of £10 to each old couple, all are at liberty to make whatever earnings they may be equal to; but no Trading whatever can be allowed upon the premises; nor any business which may interfere with the comfort of the neighbours, or be at all injurious to the premises.

VII.

Upon the death of any Husband or Wife, the survivor will be allowed, at the discretion of the Patron, to continue in possession of the house, with all its privileges; but if any Inmate shall marry again without the consent of MR. or MRS. STUART, or the Patron for the time being, he or she shall be instantly removed, and altogether deprived of the benefits of the Charity.

WILLIAM STUART.

ALDENHAM ABBEY,
February 23, 1853.

The photograph shows Mr J. Pierpont Morgan with Royal Guests at his Gannochy Estate in Scotland – August 1938. *From left to right – back row* The Hon. Elphinstone; King George VI; J. P. Morgan Jnr.; The Master of Elphinstone; Lord Elphinstone. *Centre row* – Lady Elphinstone; Queen Elizabeth; Lady Jean Elphinstone; *Front row* – the Hon. Margaret Elphinstone.

bombing campaign over London, the house was used by an evacuated maternity unit.

Then in May, 1945, Wall Hall became home to the first Emergency Teacher Training College for Women. The temporary establishment soon became a mixed College of Education and with later diversification, a College of Higher Education. Amalgamation with the closed Balls Park College (Hertford) was later followed by absorption into the Hatfield Polytechnic and its School of Education and Humanities and continued as such when the Polytechnic became the University of Hertfordshire. To consolidate its sites, the University and Wall Hall in 2003, with its Academic Staff and Students moved to new buildings in Hatfield. The Mansion and some of the related buildings were designed to provide private dwellings along with new houses, so Wall Hall enters a new phase in its long history.

REMINISCENCES OF THE GOVERNESS TO J. P. MORGAN'S CHILDREN – WRITTEN IN 1976.

… I lived at Wall Hall from mid-September to mid-December 1913; a world away from our world. I had been engaged that first year after my graduation from Radcliffe (Harvard University) as Governess – to the daughters of J. P. Morgan, Jnr. who had bought the house for his young family when he was serving his apprenticeship in banking in his family's bank in London (Morgan-Grenfell, I believe) and to which he still liked to go in the shooting season. His wife and daughters had preceded me. I went over alone on the S.S.Franconia, later as a hospital ship in World War 1, sunk in the Mediterranean. Mr Morgan came daily in the shooting season and we all returned to New York in December on the Lusitania.

I am well acquainted with my Thackeray and Jane Austen to know the lowly estate of a governess in the eyes of the British. My case was not uncomfortable. The girls were not too far away from me in age; the elder, Jane, was less than two years my junior. the younger, Frances, less than five years younger than I was. They had never been to school. They had, from very early childhood had a governess whom they adored; a cultivated French woman who had only recently had to go back to France to look after her ailing parents. Jane was already "out"; Frances had one more year in the schoolroom before "coming out". It was decided to have an English speaking governess in her last year to teach the girls the English terms in arithmetic for percentages etc., so that the girls could take care of their own bank accounts! (Also incidentally some English history and literature and a little Latin.) Frances really was "in the schoolroom" in England. She and I had all our meals there, except lunches, which we had with the family in the dining room. The schoolroom was on the third floor on the opposite side of the house from the stable yard... We could see the tower of St. Albans Abbey from the schoolroom window, framed by trees.

One of the lorries used on Church Farm – 1930 (an A.E.C. Majestic petrol engine.)

The bedrooms of the girls and myself were in an older part of the house, perhaps a part of the original farmhouse, which was reached by a door at the right of a landing part way up from the front hall... The house as I knew it was built... for Thellusson, the French banker whom Dickens, at the beginning of The Tale of Two Cities refers to as 'Tellson'. That was the time when Sir Horace Walpole and Sir Walter Scott were reviving interest in the Gothic. At Wall Hall in addition to the turrets and battlements there was an artificial "ruin", Gothic arches made of stucco, draped with English ivy. It was out beyond the grove of Scotch pines. The fact that thrilled me was that the grounds were laid out by Humphrey Repton (Amenity Repton) one of the first landscape architects, mentioned by Jane Austen in Mansfield Park which she wrote between 1811 and 1814. Repton said one should see water from the house. The River Colne was too far away, hence the canal!

I don't remember that Repton also ordered sheep, but sheep

The Home of the Aldenham Dairy Shorthorns (now the Aldenham Golf and Country Club)

there were; at the bottom of the long sloping, velvety green lawn where a fence marked the pedestrian "right of way", beyond which was the sheep pasture. It was from the schoolroom window looking towards the canal that I saw Mr. Morgan and guests shooting his "home preserve" of pheasants during a two day house party. Quite a sight when I went down to lunch; that huge circular table top, with an army of footmen circling it. As soon as a guest imbibed a dish the next was given him, so that while one was eating the entree, his opposite might be eating dessert. Hurry! Hurry! Back to the shooting! After all, it was late in the year and the days were getting short!

Within the Cow House, showing the milking bays.

WALL HALL – ALDENHAM ABBEY

Account by D. Foster – niece of one of Pierpont Morgan's staff

My great aunt, Mrs. Mary Curley, (a courtesy title as she never married,) was housekeeper at Wall Hall, as well as at Mr. Pierpont Morgan's house in Grosvenor Square, London. I was born in 1909 and spent many short holidays in Watford from 1915 onwards. I lived in Watford, where another two great aunts lived, for about two years from 1917-18 and also from 1926-28.

The house in Watford, Bushey Mill Lane, was within walking distance of Wall Hall as we usually walked over for Sunday lunch, as well as on other visits. My main memories now are of a beautiful house and magnificent gardens. We walked past Otterspool, across the park land where cattle usually grazed, to the main gate, then right past the front of Wall Hall, then left down a wide drive to a court bounded by the side of the house, the stable block topped by a large clock, the garages, laundry block, large pigeon loft etc. From the entrance door there was a hall from which a passage on the left led to the housekeeper's room, then to the Octagon room and on to the main house. On the right of the entrance hall were the servant's hall, and kitchens etc. Straight ahead was the butler's pantry, still room and large door to the library. In the housekeeper's room, one wall had two big windows looking onto the courtyard, one wall had a large coal fire, with brass fire tongs etc. it was surrounded by a brass fire guard topped with a wide red velvet covered seat. I well remember being reprimanded by Mrs. Curley for putting coal on the fire. She told me I should ring for the hall boy to do so. The other two walls of the room had various white painted cupboards and drawers. There was a large dining table and chairs. The butler always shared our meals which were luxurious and served by the kitchen staff. The butler and his wife did not live in the main house. The room was always bright with flowers and flowering plants. A large settee and armchairs had flowered washable covers.

The servant's hall was a vast room. I remember going there for the servant's Christmas dinner and dance. They had a huge Christmas tree and many presents. That same year I had a superb Christmas lunch in the Octagon room with my aunt and the butler. The inner hall from the courtyard had flagstones, very uneven. The passage from there led to the servants' hall, with a passage past the housekeeper's room, the third passage passed the butler's pantry to a green baize door opening into the library. The flower beds outside the library were often planted with heliotrope, called cherry pie, and smelt really lovely in the sunshine. The beds were always filled with flowering plants. Out beyond the walled garden there was a magnificent mulberry tree in the centre of a lawn. The tree had a circular seat around its base. Sometimes I met some of the children, presumably grand children, in the gardens and was surprised to see how plainly they were dressed. Their diet was also very plain and simple.

Around the end of the First World War, which ended in 1918. (I was nine) I remember walking in the grounds with my aunt, meeting and chatting with officers in hospital blue, accompanied by V.A.D. nurses. Part of Wall Hall was then an officers' convalescent home. I remember visits to Home Farm. The farm manager was Mr. Anderson and he and his wife were very kind and friendly, giving me Christmas presents. He took me over the farm dairy and I watched the girls making butter. He always gave me a glass full of fresh cream. I was actually taught to milk one of the cows, one of their own accredited herd.

Aunt Mary had a small boy at her beck and call. He even came

J. P. Morgan was petrified of fire. He had a staircase for him to escape from his bedroom should there be the necessity for this. On the outside wall of the Mansion (still visible) is the box where the "clocking on" device was housed. Throughout the night, the security staff had to register every time they passed by whilst on duty. Photograph by Joan Beagle.

in at intervals to make up the fire in her room. At Christmas time she had a marvellous array of presents from all the mostly London firms she dealt with on behalf of the Hall. I remember her showing me a large array of handbags etc. The servants' hall was a really large hall with an immense table in the middle, surrounded by about a dozen chairs at least. The butler took his meals with Aunt Mary when he was on duty at the Hall. The cook was in charge in the servants' hall. It was a marvellous spread, but I felt out of place as I was treated with too much respect. When I actually stayed overnight, I usually had Mrs. Morgan's lady maid's room on the first floor, next to the housekeeper's room. I remember a pink silk bed spread. During the General Strike in 1926, I listened to the news broadcast on Aunt Mary's wireless. Mrs. Morgan was ill in bed and asked me to make a note of the news and take it up to her. She gave me a £1.00 note (a huge gift in those days) She was in a large bed on a dais in the centre of a magnificent room.

Aunt Mary always had a car at her disposal, plus the services of the chauffeur. This also applied during her seaside holiday visits. I often went with her to Selfridges, Army and Navy Stores etc. She was treated with great respect by all of the different store's staff. All of the rooms in the actual Hall had beautiful china bowls of pot-pourri. I remember going round with Aunt Mary checking the flowers etc. and she stirred up the pot-pourri, with her hand. She checked that all had been done to her liking. Aunt Mary always had at least one pekingese pet. One of these was Fifi who was very fat, a very short haired small peke. Not really a very friendly one. Much of my time was spent in the lovely gardens. I used to walk through the baize door, into the library, a really magnificent room, then out through the glass doors. Facing the library was a wide lawn with shrubs and a rustic bird house on a stand. Normally I walked along the side of the house to the front, then to the right, past the winding path through the woods, down to the river. Then along a path edged with lavender bushes, to the Dell filled in the Spring with snowdrops. We often visited the greenhouses to choose grapes, fruit for the house and flowers.

In later years, I used to be a Sunday School teacher at a church in Watford. One Sunday after lunch at the Hall, Aunt Mary told the chauffeur to take me into town to Sunday school. En route, he gave me a driving lesson and I remember just missing hitting the bridge over the river at the bottom of Bushey Mill Lane! Imagine the sensation when I turned up at Church in a car! I well remember being embarrassed at arriving in a large car with a uniformed chauffeur. Unheard of in those days in our circle. Cars were only for the very rich people! The Morgan family usually came over to England for the shooting season. The staff always had their share of the pheasant and grouse. I only stayed overnight in Wall Hall if the family were away, which of course they were most of the time. My aunt was in complete charge of the household then. I always slept in the lady's maid's room. Wall Hall was a beautiful house with exquisite furnishings and pictures. There was also a marvellous assortment of china. Their house in Grosvenor Square London was really luxurious, I also stayed there. It is now part of the American Embassy. I have enjoyed remembering old days in Wall Hall.

Dorothy Foster.

Aerial view of Wall Hall, probably in the early years of the College. In the foreground is the north front with, left, Stuart's large Library. Beyond the courtyard is the stable block with its clock tower and then the walled garden as it was before the building programme of the 1960's. Photograph reproduced by permission of the University of Hertfordshire from "Our Heritage" by Tony Gardner.

THE CHEQUERS INN, ALDENHAM.

This building is now used as the Aldenham Social Club. It was probably the oldest licensed premises in the Parish. Established in 1635 by Henry Coghill of Wigbournes, (the estate which preceded Aldenham Park, now the Haberdashers' Aske's School grounds) as an inn "for the use and enjoyment of the poor," on waste land facing Aldenham Church and originally known as Church House Inn, or The Smokey House. The house was delicensed by Pierpont Morgan Jnr. when he acquired the property (as part of the Estate of Wall Hall) in 1910, and was presented to the village as a Social Centre.

The building is a three-bay timber-framed house, with queen-strut trusses and arch braces. The west gable end was originally jettied. According to Stephen Castle, the building may date from the

16th century, predating its use as an inn. The building was listed, Grade 2, in 1985.

The illustration shows the inn as it was in the first decade of the 20th century, shortly before delicensing. Note the "Tea Gardens" sign: this was very much a feature of the country inns in Edwardian days.

The Chequers Inn from the Churchyard.

A Mr. Eaton rolling the cricket pitch in front of the Aldenham Social Club.

Photograph from Mary Hood.

THE PIERPONT MORGAN LIBRARY
29 East Thirty-sixth Street
New York, N. Y. 10016

15 April 1982

Dear Mrs. Hood,

We have been very interested in your letter and will attempt to add a little to your supply of knowledge about Wall Hall.

The lease was purchased in 1910 by J. P. Morgan, the son of Pierpont Morgan, the famous nineteenth-century American banker and collector, who built the Morgan Library. In 1928, Mr. Morgan purchased the freehold outright from the Hon. A. Holland Hibbert. We have a number of early documents about the property, as well as a privately printed History of the Manor of Wall Hall and its Owners by William Page, 1930.

In this little book it is suggested that the manor was created in the late twelfth century when forests were being felled to pay the taxes required for the ransom of Richard Coeur de Lion. The first owner was said to be Guy de Walebrale or Guy de London who was probably the first resident owner. The manor is mentioned in his will dated 1218. (His son was present with King John at the signing of Magna Carta.)

In 1392, it passed into the possession of the Priory of St. Barthololmew's Smithfield (presently St. Bartholomew's Hospital), and in 1539 at the Dissolution of the Monasteries it went to the Crown. In 1544, it came into the possession of John Williams, a kinsman of Thomas Cromwell. In February 1616, there was a grant in favour of Edward Adams and Richard Amery from James I, signed by Francis Bacon. In 1667, Sir Erasmus Haily, a tenant, destroyed the manor house and chopped down the surrounding trees; it appears that he did this out of spite when he was repeatedly asked for the rent. In 1797, or thereabouts, the lease was sold to Lord Holles for 1,274 pounds; 216 acres at 10/5 per acre. In the meantime, the land was sold in 1715 and, in 1835, sold again to Mr. G. Hibbert from whose descendants Mr. Morgan bought it in 1928.

Mr. Thellusson, the tenant in 1801, rebuilt Wall Hall, planted cedar trees and laid out the grounds. In 1812, he sold the lease of Wall Hall for 28,406 pounds to Admiral Sir Charles M. Pole who fought in the American War of Independence. He renamed the manor Aldenham Abbey and built the "ruins" on the grounds. His descendants sold it to Mr. Charles Van Raalte in 1874 and in 1910 the lease was acquired by Mr. Morgan.

Mr. Morgan appointed John Fleming, a Cambridge graduate in agriculture, to be the manager of his property and I enclose a letter from him to Mr. Morgan which may interest you. We do not have any information about the "pigs that flew," but we can put you in touch with Mr. Fleming's daughter, Mrs. A. McNair, 12 Adelaid Square, Windsor, Berks. His wife is also still alive, and she may know about this episode and also about the Lord Mayor's Show in the 1920's.

We should be interested, if it is possible, to have a copy of your history of the property for our archives and we should be very interested to see your article. I hope we have been of some help.

Yours sincerely,

(Mrs.) Betty Whiddington
Assisting David Wright in
the archives of the Morgan
Library

Mrs. M. Hood
1 The Lodge - Wall Hall
Aldenham, Watford
Herts
England WD2 8AZ

ESTATE OFFICE,
WALL HALL, ALDENHAM.
WATFORD. HERTS.

December 18th, 1936.

Pierpont Morgan, Esq.
23, Wall Street,
New York, U.S.A.

Dear Mr.Morgan,

I herewith enclose the monthly statement of account. I am sorry sales have not been so good as they usually are, but November is always rather a bad month. I shall want £2,000 to carry on with. May I have this by January 6th, 1937.

I got your cable safely but up to the present I have nothing very definite to tell you about the piece of land for the school. Messrs.Rumbold and Edwards, Lord Rendlesham's Agents, are willing to put a price on the acreage of land required for the school. I understand there is to be a meeting of the Committee to discuss this question very shortly. Mr.Gibbs told me that he was under the impression that the Education Board would want from four to five acres. Anyway he is to let me know as soon as they have had a meeting and I can then find out from Rumbold & Edwards what price they will want. It has been explained to them that the land is wanted for a Church School to serve the Parish of Aldenham and Radlett. As soon as I have any definite information I will let you know.

We did quite well at the Smithfield Show in London.
Sheep - Reserve Southdown Champion, one first, 1 third and 1 fourth.
Pigs - Reserve Large White Champion and Reserve for best pair of six months old pigs in the Show, any breed, one first and one fourth prizes. Carcase Competition - Pigs second and Reserve for Bacon Carcase Championship and one fourth prize. I am glad to say also that the Champion pen of live sheep in the Show - half-breds shown by Mr.Clifton Brown, were by an Aldenham Ram. Also the Sheep carcase Champion - shown by the Northants.Farm Institute was also by an Aldenham Ram. These last two results were very satisfactory. At Watford Fat Stock Show we took 2nd. prize with a fat heifer, First and Champion with five lambs, 1st.with a fat sow and 3rd. with two bacon pigs.

Coronation Fete as for some time we did not know if there was going to be a Coronation or not, but now that everything has been settled satisfactorily we are going ahead again. I presume the alteration

J.Pierpont Morgan, Esq., Continuation Sheet No.2. 18.12.36.

in the person who is to be crowned has not made any alteration in your wishes regarding the fete. It has been rather a trying time here over it all but I am sure things will work out all right now.

I enclose a letter I had from the Methodist Church here. I have just informed them that I was sending it on to you.

There has been a lot of rain and very high wind here lately, but I do not think it has done any damage beyond taking off a few slates and tiles.

I am still bargaining over price with the Watford Electricity Department for the laying of the cable to Blackbirds Cottages and Farm. When I have prices from them and the Electricians for wiring the Farm, I will let you know.

The Harriers were here last week and found three foxes - one they killed, the second they ran to ground and the third they lost. We are expecting the fox hounds here on December 29th, so I hope they will kill somemore.

I have been trying to clear up the sale of the two Percheron Mares to Lord Carnegie. It has not been at all a satisfactory deal as they were both right and straight in every way when they were sent off. He says one is vicious and kicks and will not pay for her - in fact he has not paid in full for the other. I have written him that if he pays me for the one he wants to keep and the carriage I will take the other back. At the moment that is where the matter rests. I do not think I shall want to sell him anything again.

We had the misfortune to lose the old white bull. He got down in his box at night and got wedged and could not get up and in his struggles broke his back. He is a great loss.

Everything else seems to be going on all right.

With good wishes for Xmas and the New Year.

Yours sincerely,

John Fleming

CHAPTER 2

THE BUILDINGS OF WALL HALL

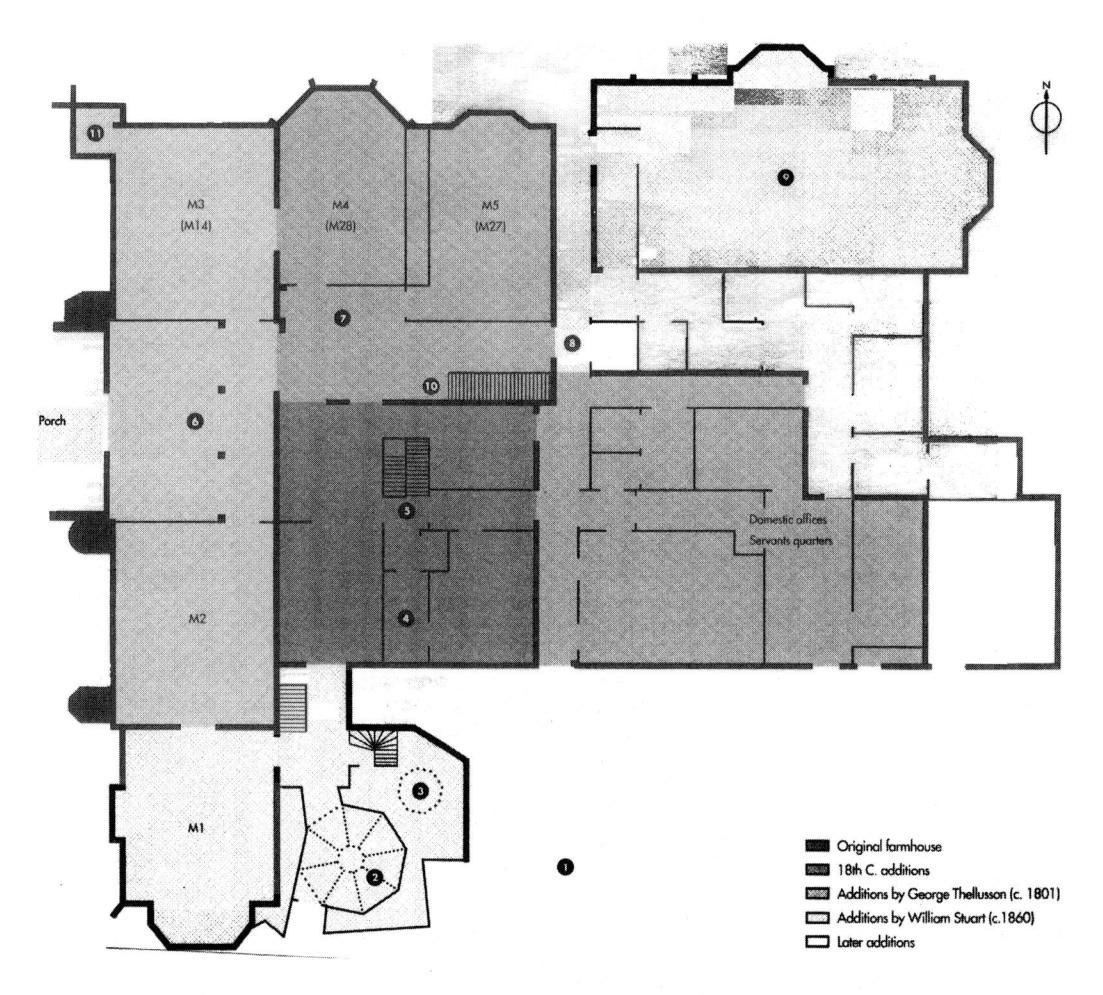

Key to features Ground floor – 1. Stable courtyard; 2. Octagon; 3. Strong room; 4. Housekeeper's room; 5. Stairs to cellars; 6. Entrance hall; 7. Inner hall; 8. Back corridor; 9. Large library; 10. Main staircase; M1. Dining room; M2. Small library; M3. Drawing room; M4. Bowed drawing room; M5. Billiard room.

First floor – 11. Fire escape; M14. J.P. Morgan's bedroom; Second floor – M27. Night nursery; M28. Day nursery.
Reproduced by permission of Hertfordshire University Press from *Our Heritage* by Tony Gardner.

A book plate c1800

THE MANSION OF WALL HALL

Copies sent to Mr.T.F.May and Mr.Perkins
From – K.J.Ming, (a part-time student) 4th December 1980.
Initial consideration of the development of the house.

The house can be divided into 7 major parts.

(1) Original? (Figures 4 and 5) a three storey and cellar house. It is interesting that this is aligned accurately to the points of the compass, and at an angle to the stableblock.

(2) Extension to the back (or front) of 1. (figures 7 and 10.)

(3) New West front block castellated – North front castellated to match (notice of sale in 1812 indicates fronts.) This house, shown in phase 3 (number 6) is presumably the Thellusson house. The 1841 book plate perhaps also shows this phase. If the engraving represents reality, the ground floor has a cloister like room on either side of the front door on the West front. The spiral staircase (figure 11) also appears to be in existance in engraving on the N.W. corner. Assume about 1800.

(4) The Ballroom (?) extension – single storey (*figure 9*)

(5) This is almost a separate building, only connected at the ground floor. It is red brick, and requires further investigation to determine to which phase it belongs. (*figures M1, 2 and 3.*)

(6) An extension to the the West front, in the style of the remainder, but not appearing in the 1841 book plate.

(7) Single storey construction (*figure 8 and 9*) filling gap between 7 and domestic quarters and appearing, from the plans to be later than both.

Assuming above to be substantially correct, five phases of the development of the house can be identified as shown in the sketch. These assumptions now have to be confirmed (or revised) and the sequence and dating to be established using the following sources:
1. Style, construction, fittings etc.
2. Structural clues.
3. Engravings and photographs of the house.
4. Maps and plans.
5. Any other records.

THE BUILDINGS OF WALL HALL

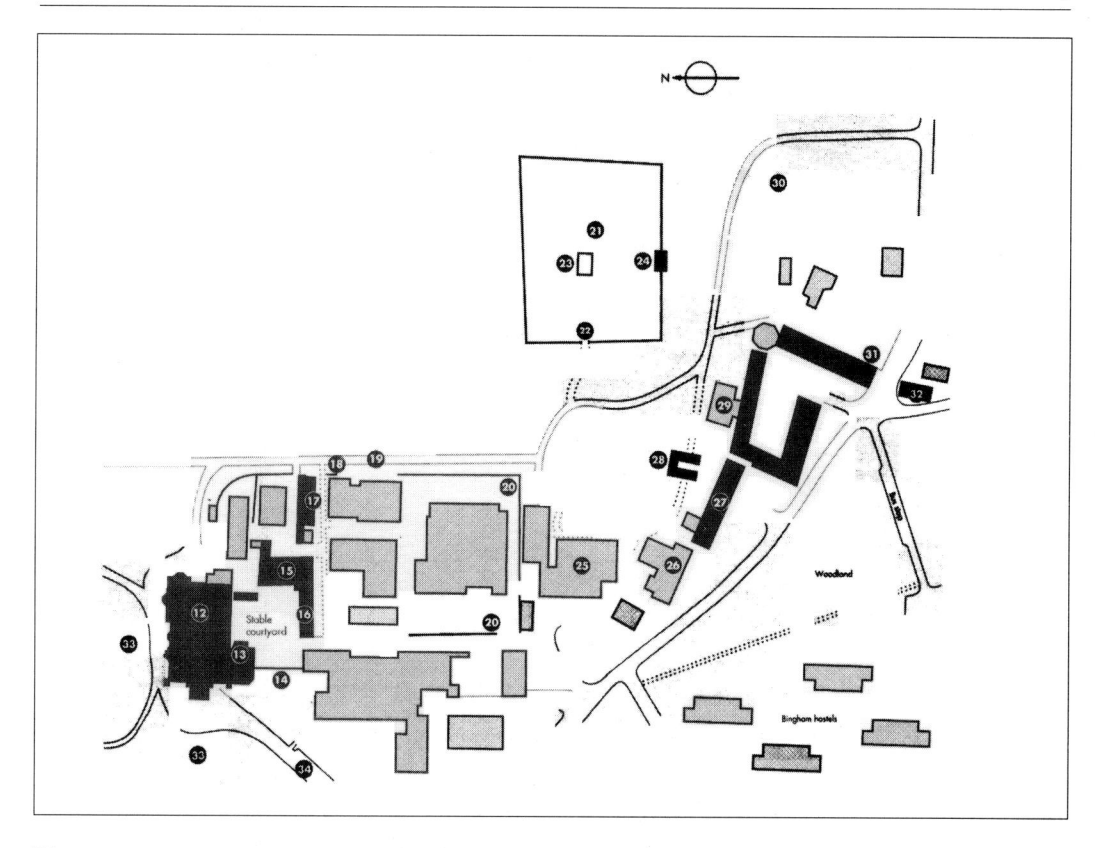

■ Original buildings.
☐ Additions by Wall Hall College & University of Hertfordshire.

Key to features – 12. Mansion; 13. Octagon; 14. Orangery wall; 15. South hostel; 16. Stable block; 17. Glasshouse; 18. Wrought iron gate; 19. Broad walk; 20. Old garden wall; 21. Italian garden; 22. Wrought iron gate; 23. Lily pond; 24. Love seat; 25. Library and computer centre; 26. Science and geography; 27. Holbrook; 28. Folly; 29. Art department; 30. Ice house; 31. Farmhouse; 32. Old barn; 33. Cedars; 34. way to Otterspool.

Reproduced by permission of Hertfordshire University Press from *Our Heritage* by Tony Gardner.

CHAPTER 3

DISCUSSION DOCUMENTS – PURCHASE OF ESTATE

HERTFORDSHIRE COUNTY COUNCIL EDUCATION
WALL HALL ESTATE

A discussion document re: the purchase of Wall Hall.

Finance and general purposes Sub-Committee. Meeting 3rd. January 1944

The County Council at their meeting in February, 1943, approved the recommendation of the Education Committee that a house should be acquired for use as a conference centre for refresher courses for teachers and youth leaders and as a residential centre for adult education. At their meeting in November 1943 they decided in the event of notice to exercise the Council's option being received, to purchase Wall Hall Estate and Mansion at Aldenham, belonging to the late Mr J. P. Morgan and passed the following resolution:

> That the said purchase be carried out under the provisions of Section 14 of the Hertfordshire County Council Act, 1935, which empowers the Council to acquire land for the purpose of preserving the same as an open space or for the preventing or regulating the erection of buildings thereon, but that in respect of any portion agreed between the Town Planning and Education Committees to be purchased or appropriated for educational purposes (which the said Committees are hereby empowered to agree) such portion be purchased or appropriated under the provisions of the Education Acts for educational purposes accordingly.

The Committee may thus be presented with the unique opportunity of obtaining for educational purposes a house and grounds centrally situated in the County which, with few alterations, is admirably suited as a residential college. It is suggested that they should consider both a short-term and a long-term policy for its use.

SHORT TERM POLICY. TRAINING OF TEACHERS.

As the Committee are aware, the President of the Board of Education has already announced that in order to train men and women from the fighting services to take their places as teachers after the war it will be necessary for the Board to work through a number of Local Education Authorities. Informal conversations with senior officials of the Board of Education have taken place and it is possible to say that the Board consider Hertfordshire one of the authorities whom they would wish to assist them in the task of training teachers after the war, and that they would like the possibility of using Wall Hall for the purpose to be considered. The National plan, envisaged by the Board includes certain training centres being given a bias for different types of education and, having regard to its situation, it is probable that at Wall Hall the County Council would be asked to specialize in the training of teachers in rural science, handicrafts and horticulture. The County Council would act as the Board's agents and the whole cost of the scheme (including current loan charges) would be carried by the Board. Although it is impossible to say exactly when the training should begin the Board are anxious that plans should be prepared without delay and the possibility of opening the College next Autumn should be definitely considered. The use of Wall Hall for this purpose would not directly assist Education in Hertfordshire, although there would be many indirect benefits. In the first place the Education Committee could no doubt use the premises by arrangement during the holidays for their own purposes and it would be possible in designing the curriculum to arrange for many joint activities for the benefit both of the trainees and of Hertfordshire teachers. Moreover, although Wall Hall would be training teachers for the whole country, it should be possible for the County Council to have certain advantages in selecting teachers whom they had trained for work in Hertfordshire. The fact that Hertfordshire would not be the main beneficiary should not, however, weigh too much with the Committee, as it is clear that the national policy can only be carried out if a number of Educational Authorities are prepared to play their part in its fulfilment. It is, in fact, something of an honour that Hertfordshire has been asked to be one of the few authorities co-operating in the scheme.

LONG TERM POLICY. ADULT EDUCATION.

"It is one for the profoundest tragedies of our national life today that everywhere the cry is for competency to meet new problems and nowhere is that competency to be found. Ability we have in abundance, but it has never had time to learn. In large part this is due to the inadequacy of our education for the young; but in part also it is due to our neglect to offer real opportunity for education of the adult."

H. C. Dent: *A New Order in English Education.*

The White Paper stresses more than once the fact that education is a continuing process which does not finish when the child leaves school and suggests that Local Education Authorities should make provision for Adult Education on a scale as yet unknown in this country. Hertfordshire, although forward in many types of educational provision, has not yet given Adult Education the attention it deserves. There are approximately 500,000 men and women aged 18 and over in the County, and the total expenditure for Adult Education on the annual Educational estimates during the last ten years has never exceeded £2,165 or less than 1d. per head of population. The problem will have to be tackled in various ways and over many years, but the purchase of Wall Hall would provide an excellent opportunity which, if taken, would not only enrich the spiritual and cultural life of the County, but be an example to the whole country. It is suggested that, when the immediate task of training teachers has been accomplished, the house should be used for a twofold purpose. In the first place as a centre for providing our own teachers with opportunities for cultural education, and in the second place as a residential college for both long and short courses in every range of educational activity, cultural, technical and vocational and open to all residents in the County. Coleg Harlech, Newbattle Abbey and Woodbroke have, on a limited scale, already proved the success of this form of continued education, but no local education authority have yet had the opportunity, now presented to the Committee.

It is a platitude to say that the teachers are the most important factor in the success or failure of a school, but in the past it has not always been realised that their efficiency can only be maintained if they are given regular opportunities for intellectual recreation. The

County Council spend approximately £600,000 a year on teachers' salaries or about 60 per cent of the total amount spent on Education and only £165 on Refresher Courses. At its lowest this is a false economy, for to get the maximum effective contribution from teachers is the most economical way of getting value for the considerable sum spent on salaries. Wall Hall could be used continually during the school holidays and, indeed, during the long week-ends in term time as a centre for giving Hertfordshire teachers the opportunity of reading and studying, of learning the latest and most modern methods of teaching practice, and of experimenting in new techniques, particularly in the practical subjects of physical training, handicrafts, domestic science and rural sciences. It is not too much to say that it could become a power-house radiating encouragement and inspiration to the 2,000 teachers in the Committee's service and its influence on the quality of their teaching cannot be measured.

Parallel and to some extent interrelated with this function would be its use for Conference purposes and as a centre for Adult Education. Many of the Committee will have read the work of the Danish People's High Schools described recently by the President of Corpus Christi, Oxford, in his "The Future of Education." Sir Richard Livingstone argues that the provision of residential Adult Education should not be limited to the tiny fraction of the population who are able to enjoy a university education and argues from the limited experience of this country and very considerable experience of the Scandinavian states that these opportunities should be extended. His ideas have received powerful support not only from the Scott Committee on land utilization in rural areas, but in the post-war proposals of the Workers' Educational Association and the Trades Union Council. The latter urge that, in addition to residential colleges taking adult students for longer periods, "the most serious consideration ought to be given to the possibility of instituting in this country a system of short-term residential courses, widely available, which would help to build up a social consciousness amongst the young citizens of the country, and might well be the means of establishing a permanent interest in adult education amongst a much wider section of the community than is touched by the provision hitherto made. The Government" they say "should give a lead to employers to release their workers for this kind of short course, with an assurance of reinstatement on their return."

There is also an increasing awareness among the employers of labour that if they are to find sufficient men and women to fill the more responsible posts in their factories and workshops there must be an extension of general education in addition to anything that is done of a technical nature. At the moment, this education is gained largely through classes attended in the evenings at the end of the working day and this is a slow and tedious, uncertain business. Both teacher and taught not infrequently go tired to their studies, the short time each class lasts and long intervals between classes prevent effective concentration, and occasional absences are inevitable. The same amount of knowledge which is at present gained by this method could be obtained with much better results by a period of full-time study of approximately three months.

Wall Hall could provide weekend, weekly, monthly and even longer courses in a wide range of subjects and to mix teachers and men and momen in other occupations would be to their mutual advantage. Moreover, thought will have to be given to the content of the studies and this report does not pretend to do more than outline a general policy for the Committee's consideration.

HOUSE AND GARDENS

It has been suggested that Wall Hall should concentrate on the training of teachers for country schools and the gardens will play an essential part in their training. As the Committee are aware, increasing emphasis is now placed on making the curriculum in rural schools relative to the experience of the children and to the type of life that they will ultimately lead. In order to train teachers to take their part in this work, which includes practical nature study, field ecology, biology, horticulture, farm visits, survey making and local geography, a well developed garden would be invaluable and would provide examples of attractive planning, experimental and demonstration plots for fruit and vegetables; botanical plots; teaching collections of grasses, legumes, trees, flowering shrubs, herbacious plants, greenhouse and frame management etc. In addition, there will have to be an adequate laboratory for the more academic side of this instruction. Fortunately, Wall Hall is well endowed with the facilities necessary and with little adaption could be used for this purpose.

The garden is equipped with a number of hot-houses designed

for the production of luxury fruits and flowers and it might be possible to arrange for these to be let to a commercial grower.

In order that students may be properly trained it will be necessary for them to obtain teaching practice in these subjects and something in the nature of a Practising School with a horticultural bias will be essential. It would be possible to arrange for a group of approximately 40 boys to undertake a course of this nature. Some would be day boys but accomodation is available for 16–20 boarders. It is sometimes forgotten that agriculture is still the largest single industry in Hertfordshire and it is increasingly important that provision should be made for the instruction of boys who are going to make it their career.

An experiment of this type would fit in well with the proposals for technical education contained in the White Paper and the experience gained would enable the Committee to frame a wider policy for instruction of this nature.

The scheme has a twofold merit in that while providing technical instruction for a number of boys, it will also play an essential part in the training of student teachers and in the Refresher Courses for teachers.

CONCLUSION

If both the short-term policy of the training of demobilized teachers and the long-term policy of Wall Hall eventually becoming a House of Education are to be fulfilled, there are certain administrative decisions to be made which are of vital importance. Sufficient land must be acquired round the house itself to ensure adequate playing-fields and opportunities for recreational activities which will be an essential part of the training of teachers and students, and it will also be required for training boys in horticulture – outlined earlier in the Report. The furniture and equipment must be simple, dignified and well designed; there must be an adequate library and, above all, the Staff must be picked with the greatest discrimination. On the Warden eventually appointed, the success of the House will largely depend and the Committee will have to be prepared to pay a salary that will attract first-rate ability. In the meantime, if the House is to be ready for the date when the Board suggest, it should be available for the training of teachers and if the Staff are to be selected and trained, it is not too early for the Committee to consider the recommendations appended in this report.

The following letter has been addressed by the President of the Board of Education to the Chairman:

Board of Education,
14 Belgrave Square,
London, s.w.1.
8th December 1943.

Dear Alderman Williams,

I have been interested to hear of the purchase by the Hertfordshire County Council of the Pierpont Morgan estate and of the proposal that the house should be used as a centre for Adult Education. This seems to me a valuable move and your Authority are to be congratulated upon it.

You are, in fact, giving a lead in the development of Adult Education on what to Local Education Authorities are new lines.

I gather that you will be willing to consider making the house available for a period, if suitable, for our proposed emergency scheme for the training of teachers. I need hardly say that help of this kind will be very welcome.
    Yours sincerely,
     (Signed) R.A.Butler.

Recommendation: That subject to the completion of the purchase of Wall Hall by the County Council, the house and immediated grounds be used for the training of teachers and general education purposes.

Adopted.

H.C.C. FURTHER EDUCATION SUB-COMMITTEE.
MEETING 13TH SEPTEMBER 1946.
WALL HALL EMERGENCY TRAINING COLLEGE.

In May of this year the first batch of Wall Hall students completed their year's course. Ninety eight students had been admitted at the beginning of the course and three more were admitted shortly afterwards. During the course, ten students withdrew, either at the suggestion of the college authorities or because they themselves decided they were unsuited for the teaching profession. Three students have been referred for an extra term. All the other students have obtained posts before the end of the college session.

The age range of the students was from 21–41 years, the average age being 27 years. 76 per cent of them had Grammar School education and 48 per cent had passed the School Certificate. Of the remainder, half had been to a Commercial or Central school and the rest had left an Elementary school at 14 years of age. They came from a variety of previous occupations: 16 had been wardens in War-time Nurseries, 8 had been in the Land Army, 2 were unqualified teachers, and the rest had been in factories, offices, shops, banks and hostels. Only 5 of them had been in the Forces. It is interesting to compare these students with the second batch who began in August. There are 128 students on the second course, 46 of whom were previously in the Forces and 23 have been Wardens in War-time Nurseries. The rest come from as wide a variety of jobs as last year's students. 78 per cent of them have had a Grammar School education, but only 38 per cent have gained their School Certificate.

Those who have met and talked with Wall Hall students have lost their fear that the Emergency Training Scheme might mean a lowering of standards in the teaching profession. The quality of the students is first rate. They have a maturity of outlook and soundness of judgment rarely met with in students at ordinary Training Colleges. To train for a new career in the thirties or late twenties is a task not lightly to be undertaken. The students have thought seriously before embarking on the course and the majority of them are whole-heartedly determined to make a success of the new venture. Although many of them have been out of touch with book learning for years, their experience and maturity have made up for the lack or break in their formal education. Their approach is more practical and realistic than is usual in 18 year old students and their keenness has helped them to cover ground far more quickly. With them, teaching is a vocation and they are going into the schools with almost missionary zeal, but with a zeal which age and experience has tempered with discretion. The success of a scheme depends not only on them, but on the rest of the teaching profession. If they are to be accepted as equals by other teachers, then their freshness and realism will infuse new life into the schools. If they are cold-shouldered, they may lose their enthusiasm and the schools will be the poorer for the loss.

HERTFORDSHIRE COUNTY COUNCIL WALL HALL EMERGENCY TRAINING COLLEGE – 1947.

The County Council approved the purchase of the Wall Hall house and immediate grounds for educational purposes in 1943 and shortly afterwards the Ministry of Education suggested that it should be used as an Emergency Training College for women teachers. It was opened for this purpose in the Spring of 1945.

It is not intended that the Emergency Scheme for training should continue for more than another couple of years, and it would soon have been necessary for the Committee to have considered the future of the buildings. A situation has arisen however, which necessitates an immediate decision.

The Principal of the College, Miss K. M. Balfern, has accepted the post of Principal of the Brighton Training College and, after consultation with the Ministry of Education, it became evident that the chance of securing a suitable Principal for the remaining two sessions would be remote. If, however, Wall Hall was to be run eventually as a Permanent Training College, it would be possible to find a Principal who would be prepared to accept responsibility for the Emergency Training College if she was subsequently to continue as head of the permanent institution. The Ministry of Education have also been reviewing the general position for the permanent training of teachers and have decided that there is scope for another Training College of this type for women teachers in Primary schools and that there are notable advantages in establishing such a College at Wall Hall. The building has been specifically adapted for this purpose at considerable expense, there is already a strong association between the schools in that part of the County and there is a nucleus of a professional and domestic staff who would be prepared to continue.

If the Committee agreed to the Ministry's proposal, the eventual cost of the Permanent Training College would be on the same basis as that at Balls Park, i.e. the whole cost of maintaining the College would be charged to the Ministry of Education and divided by them in proportion among all Local Education Authorities.

Under the circumstances, the Urgency Committee decided to notify the Ministry that the County Council are prepared to establish a Permanent Training College for Women teachers at Wall Hall when it ceases to establish as an Emergency Training College. The post of Principal having been advertised, the Committee subsequently interviewed short-listed applicants and appointed Miss I. N. Dickinson, B.A.

CHAPTER 4

THE EARLY YEARS OF THE COLLEGE

My first encounter with the Wall Hall Estate was in 1942. Cycling from Mill Hill to Chipperfield for a brief holiday, I left the A41 and was eating a sandwich on the edge of a lovely woodland path, when a voice called "What are you doing? Private property. If I thought it was a rabbit I should shoot!" Thus the game-keeper in the Otterspool woods! There was no M1, no college, but the Mansion, owned until that year, by the American millionaire, J. Pierpont Morgan, was being used for hush-hush training for one of the armed forces, and possibly for housing high ranking prisoners.

In the Autumn of 1944, when the County Council had acquired the whole estate – the embryo of the present college was born. The intensive 13 month courses for people of wide experience, produced many fine primary school teachers. A break with tradition was inevitable as unusual buildings, few resources, wartime rationing, blackout and lack of transport, demanded endless improvisation and the quest for an imaginative approach from these 'mature' students and from the specially selected tutors. The challenge must have been enormous.

The County Education Officer, later knighted for his services to education, was a man of extraordinary vitality, vision, courage and opportunism and he backed his brain-child to the hilt. the Board of Education recruited the students and appointed the principal and Tutors. the County provided the setting – the Mansion, mock Gothic, encasing an old farm house (a story traceable back to the Domesday Book) its yard bordered by laundry rooms and stables with the lovely clock tower, all looking down on a boiler house and workshop and a row of new greenhouses masked from the front of the house by the Gothic glass screen of the one time Orangery. These houses were full of amaryllis, cyclamen and ferns of every kind for use in display, on tables or before the mirrors, as in the entrance hall. The nearest of the greenhouses was fashioned as a Grotto and a door led into the gold and white dining room, first used as a music and lecture room. The double doors opened into the drawing room, the walls of which were covered from floor to ceiling with an enchanting Chinese wallpaper. It was sold for a song, but the elaborately moulded gold and white ceiling remained. Sadly, as each of the first and second floor rooms had to serve as dormitories for 4–6 students of mature years, that ceiling collapsed and all that was rescued was the cornice! The master bedroom, at the head of the red carpeted staircase, had not only an emergency control switch for all the main lights, but also a spiral escape route down from the small turret to the garden.

Of the other buildings available for residential or educational use, were the Morgan garages which converted neatly into a science laboratory and small geography room. Of outstanding interest, naturally was the 18th. century coaching inn, Otterspool House, with its otters pool, and the Colne river running the length of the garden swept by two immense beech trees. The drive ran in straight line into Watford and up the valley, the old coach road made its way to St. Albans and is said to figure in 'Cobbett's Rural Rides.' The house had many attractive features, but of special interest were the lovely Delft tiles in the hall and the gracious drawing room where the rich tradition of the Art department began.

The estate offered a wealth of natural and historic interest. The 37 acres or garden landscaped in accordance with 19th. century fashion, offered, not only superb cedars and other trees, but a convincing Gothic folly and classical summerhouse, damaged by fire bombs, an ice house, and a series of lily ponds, linked by a cascade which, when frozen in Winter, provided excellent skating. The sinking of water bores and of a 30U pipe-line to supply water to new towns, drained the ponds forever.

Nearer the Mansion, were the two walled gardens where peaches, nectarines, figs and medlars grew. Shaggy palm trees and the little fountain, now in the farm courtyard, added an exotic touch. Carefully tended vines and out of season fruits flourished in the numerous hothouses. These served as craft rooms for years to come. The Head Gardener was said to have £2,000 annually to spend as he thought fit, and even J. P. M. could not enter the greenhouses unless unlocked by him. It was against this setting and in the

Gothic Hall added to the house in 1870, that on May 15th. 1945, the late Lord Butler formally declared Wall Hall College open and gave it his blessing.

PERSONALITIES.

In 1945, there were unforgettable personalities on the Estate, all of whom enriched, to a greater or lesser extent, the quality of experience for every resident in the College. The portly, dignified figure of Mr Bingley, the Butler, who lived at the entrance gate, in Aldenham Village; next door to him, the quiet, philosophical semi-retired Gardener, Mr Hart senior and his wife; Mrs. Sharpe, the Verger's wife, who had been a lady's maid at Wall Hall, and who worked for the rest of her life as part-time seamstress for the College giving invaluable help during the period of make do and mend, fashioning curtains, chair covers or aprons for the domestic staff from dust sheets or fabrics left behind after the sale. At Otterspool Lodge lived Mr Steward the Head Gardener, a friend of the Head Gardener at Blenheim Palace. He had kept the greenhouses going throughout the war and had himself been a victim of 'gas' during the 1914–18 War.

Better known to many were Mr and Mrs. Weeks who for many years cared devotedly for the gardens and fabric of Otterspool House. Residents of Otterspool will remember, with affection, their kindness, sense of humour and constant care. Mrs. Weeks, now nearly 100 years old but in full possession of her mental faculties, lives in a Home in Watford and affirms, with a twinkle, that of course, she was accustomed to working with 'gentry.'

Then there was Mr Gibbs, who now lives in Radlett. Quiet, efficient and greatly respected by all, he was deputy to Mr Fred Hart and responsible especially for the heating. He was a fine cricketer and had often played on the Wall Hall cricket field.

Finally, Mr Fred Hart, with his wife Ethel, who, after 50 years service on the Estate, now lives in privileged accommodation, in Aldenham. In earlier days, Mr Hart had been chauffeur to Pierpont Morgan and had driven the family to their house in Park Lane, or to 'shoots' in Scotland. Among his passengers were many distinguished guests including Royalty. During the war, the Harts looked after Wall Hall and Mr Hart served as a member of the war-time emergency fire service. He became Chief Maintenance Engineer when the County Council established the College, and with the motto 'We must change with the times' he became its priceless gift from the past. Apart from being a perfect driver, who had to content himself (in 1945) with driving an old army ambulance, he had a complete knowledge of the lay-out of every building, every cable, every drain. He was so gifted a craftsman that there was nothing that he could not turn his hand to, from painting to plumbing to every skilled repair or the making of props for stage use. he was, in every sense a pillar of Wall Hall and one of its greatest friends.

Miss Kathleen Balfern.
The first Principal.

CHAPTER 4A

MISS A. K. DAVIES'S TALK WITH JOHN NEWSOM

(An explanation from Miss A. K. Davies about the following transcript:)

SIR JOHN NEWSOM, former Education Officer for Hertfordshire, came and stayed at Wall Hall on the 29th. November 1968. I took the opportunity of asking him about the early days of the College and the conversation was either taped, or one of the secretaries sat in and took notes. (I can't remember which.) I showed the subsequent typescript to Miss Dickinson, who made a few comments, indicated in the footnotes at the bottom of the pages.)

K.D. I understand that the County Council had an option on the house. Was this pre-war?

J.N. Yes, that was just before the war – just about when I came.

K.D.. Do you remeber how or why?

J.N. Yes. You see in those days the Town Planning Legislation was very different from now and the County Council could see Watford growing and expanding in virtually an uncontrolled way and they thought that if we can buy the Morgan estate in due course – we know it's all right now – Morgan will never sell it for building land, and if we buy it, we can protect the eastern side of Watford from expansion and keep it with a rural lung, and it was on what might be called sound primitive town planning motives that the option was taken up. Well, of course, this was done before the war and that was when the County Council first came onto the scene. Then when Morgan died, I think it was in 1942 or 3, they were faced with taking up the option. They had paid out quite a nominal sum, about £2,000 I think, which is more now but it was still very small, they were faced, in the middle of a war, with should they pay out a lot of money – I forget what the actual figure was, but that could be obtained from the records, but it was something like £100,000 which would now be very much more of course; and there was a great debate in the County Council and, in fact, it was one of those times when the County Council, in my 18 years of their service, rose to quite a high level of debate, because it was difficult to say in the middle of a war why you should spend all that money on acquiring some land; it was much easier to say, well, we have put down £2,000 and we have lost it. But a number of people got up and said to the effect that if we win this war, then this will be enormously important and if we lose, it doesn't matter, and it went through, and what they also did was they said, as we cannot spend money on many other things, we must pay this off as quickly as we can; don't let's spread it over 60 years, let's stick something on the rates, on the whole County, to get this paid off quickly, and a man called Alderman Goddard, who only died recently at a vast age – he was a very old man then – he happened, I think, to be Chairman of the appropriate committee, and what became known as the Goddard tuppence, was really the extra money for paying for Wall Hall Estate. Well, the whole lot would have fallen on the County Council, on the rate payers of Hertfordshire, unless one could find some use for part of the land and the house or houses, because there were the farms, which would rank for a government grant, and the Clerk of the County Council, then a man called Elton Longmore, summoned me to his presence and said, can you think of any educational reason, anything you could use that house for, because if you can, we may be able to get the Board of Education, as it then was, to agree to put up some money. Well, I didn't need much time or trouble for me to think of all sorts of things that we could do with it. In fact, we first thought of it as a residential education centre. We knew we could not use it until after the war, but after the war a residential adult education centre – and indeed it was on that basis that the original negotiations began, but they were a bit sticky, I mean the Ministry were not likely to let us charge part of the cost for a post-war educational institution, and then very fortunately the preliminaries on what eventually became the emergency training scheme began. They began quite a long time before the end of the war, in 1943.

J.N. That came from the Ministry.

K.D.. Butler, at that time?

J.N. Butler was the President of the Board of Education. A man called Fleming, who eventually became the Permanent Secretary, was the Assistant Secretary in charge of it, and another man called S. H. Wood was the sort of inspiration in terms of thinking. He eventually became Secretary of the McNair Committee for the training of teachers, but I remember ringing up the Department and saying, look, if you want Hertfordshire to be one of the participants in this emergency training scheme, I've got a house going which, with a very modest expenditure, could make at least a small college, and unlike present methods, I got an O.K. back the same afternoon. Well, having got that, then the Clerk of the County Council readily agreed. Meanwhile, the house had been requisitioned by the Government and the first time I ever came here myself, it was being used as the headquarters of some branch of clandestine warfare in North East Europe and so the security here was extremely strong and you weren't allowed in the whole building and were only allowed in with somebody with you all of the time, and only very cursorily, and there were things like pistol ranges in the garden* and places where bombs and explosives could be tried out and big motor cars. It was very much James Bond in a way; big motor cars used to arrive in the middle of the night from airfields and people got out of Europe or people used to leave from an aerodrome not very far from here to be dropped in Europe. I think myself – I strongly suspect that it was mainly Holland and Belgium they were operating because although the security was very good, when I went into the Mess, the ante-room to the mess, and dined with them and lunched with them, all the clandestine newspapers were out on the table and this revealed in the language that they were in what was going on in a way; I mean, not that I could understand them, but I just knew enough to know that they were Dutch or Flemmish. Well, then when the invasion of Europe came in June 1944, it shut down for that, because it moved over, of course, much nearer the front line; indeed, this sort of thing changed character altogether.

Then it had a brief period as an emergency maternity home, a maternity home out of London because at that time, too, V1

---

* Pistol range in the Dell, now an open air theatre. It was said that Hesse was here.

bombs were falling in London and there was a secondary evacuation from London in the autumn of 1944, especially of people – hospitals and cases – and this was rapidly turned into a very ropey sort of maternity home and a labour ward was established up, I think, in what is, well –

K.D. Now my bedroom.

J.N. I think probably your bedroom, because it was all painted bright white and there were sluices – all sorts of things, special apparatus – and I remember coming here during that period. Of course- I was beginning to come occasionally and have a look at what we might have to do, and hearing the screams of small children, I mean really tiny babies; so there are people who have got place of birth "Wall Hall" on their certificates or things now. Then eventually these people packed up – they got out before the war was over, because we managed to have our first conference of educational staff here, in the most primitive conditions, in the spring of 1945, before the war was over. We were under tremendous pressure to get the Emergency Training College started and indeed we had to get it started from a house that had been used as a maternity home, before that a centre of skulduggery, we had to get it ready to open in three months which – and when you come to think of the shortages of manpower and equipment and everything; everything had to be just ordinary Office of Works stuff, some of which lasted for a long time. You may still have got some of it in the building.

K.D. Oh, yes, we have.

J.N. However, we came in – I can still remember a conference which Alan Chorlton, who is now Education Officer for Oxfordshire, he was my deputy then – and there was no heating in the place at all and this was winter, it must have been Christmas 1944, we sat with overcoats and mufflers in that first big room on the right as you come in the main door, and talked about post-war school building and how we were going to get new schools built, and so on and so forth. As I say, the war was still on. However, by the Spring of 1945, the place was opened with, I think, about 100 women. Not many of them had come out of the services; the war in Europe was just about to be over but, of course, it wasn't over in the Far East -

K.D. May, 1945.

J.N. May, '45 and indeed there should be in your archives – I know

I've got one at home in mine – a photograph of Mr Butler at the opening ceremony standing outside actually talking to me. But that was in May 1945. We used to say we were the first college opened* we were certainly the first womens' college. I think a few weeks before, another one opened in the Midlands, in Coventry or somewhere. We both used to look upon ourselves as at least among the first two or three; and that is, in a way, how it began. Well then, it never really grew very much while it was an Emergency Training College but we did certain extensions and got about another 30 or 40 girls in very hugger-mugger, some of them having to live out, and after about – whatever it was, it was quite a short life as an Emergency Training College, it was about three years** I think, certainly no…

K.D. Yes.

J.N. I don't think it had more than three lots through, but that can be seen from the Minutes and things. Then the battle began again. I mean, was it going back to be an adult education place or should we, having started it off as a College of Education or training College, as it was then called, and having got a start, wouldn't it be barmy not to make it a permanent college if the Government wanted it. Wel…

K.D. You had presumably, already opened Balls Park at this time.

J.N. Just about. Balls Park was 1947 – because Miss Joachim, who was the Vice-Principal, went to be Vice-Principal of Balls Park when it opened, and she's now up in Durham, Neville's Cross I think,…

K.D. St. Hilds.

J.N St. Hilds, yes. Well, then Miss Balfern, who had been the first Principal, who had come from Brighton – no.…

K.D. Went to Brighton.

J.N. Yes, I don't know where she came from…

K.D.. Was it somewhere in the West, Bristol or Bath, or…

J.N. I don't know. I think she may have been in teaching. I only remember that the appointment was a joint appointment between the Ministry and ourselves, which really meant it was the Ministry, because they were paying for the whole lot.

* This was the first college opened; another college had opened an experimental wing earlier.
** There were five intakes, courses lasting 13 months with 8 weeks between.

J.N As a courtesy, I was asked to go up and interview Miss Balfern up at the Department and I said well, let's go out and see the College – she had never seen it, and we were driving out through North London and through the outskirts of Hendon, when she pointed to a traditional primary school on the right and said, "That's where I first started teaching some years ago."

K.D. Oh, yes.

J.N. And then she came out here. Well, then when Brighton came up and before we had made up our minds – this was when Freda Gwilliam left Brighton and has been for the last 20 years or more, the Chief Woman Advisor to the Colonial Office – we couldn't say to Miss Balfern, quite apart from whether we wanted to, we can really offer you a permanent job. I'm afraid, well I say afraid, I've never regretted my advice, I said, I think you ought to, if you can get Brighton, get it. Then you've something absolutely safe, because I had, in fact, got up my sleeve, in my own mind,[*] the fact that Nancy Dickinson, who was the Joint Divisional Education Officer[†] with another, and that was Kenneth Spreadbury, for South west Herts. would make an admirable head of college, who had all the right qualities, I thought, but she had no experience of anything like this in the world at all. She had been a modern language specialist in a grammar school and then had been doing admin. for three or four years. But she was a most competent teacher and a competent administrator. This is, in a way, what the head of a training college ought to be. And so Nancy really walked in, I mean, we saw what she did; and then, of course, the developments began; it became a permanent college and developed, and things happened dramatically, especially in the last ten years, I mean since I had anything to do with it, and great development happened after I left. But there are one or two rather amusing little aside things. When we first came round, you see, the place was full of furniture…

K.D. Of tremendous value I should imagine.

J.N. Well, some of it was very valuable and some of Morgan's stuff from other places in England had been grouped here. I think he

---

[*] The post was advertised, about six candidates were interviewed at County Hall.
[†] Was joint with Mr. Colville Brown, who subsequently went to RIBA and now is RNIB K.S. was the third (ex R.A.F and given charge of Further Education.)

had a big house in Scotland too, but it was an enormous jumble; I mean, I remember seeing an original Raeburn portrait and next to it, a Raeburn worked in wool by Mrs. Pierpont Morgan, and anyone who could hang on a wall these two things next to each other had, I thought, a rather odd view. But some of the furniture was superb and we ought to have kept it but the County Council, you see, at that time thought well, we've had to pay all this money, let's get as much back as we can and really it was very short-sighted because we sold off this very good furniture which was of the size for a house of this sort and got quite a good price for it – not an awful lot, because people didn't want such big furniture then –

K.D. And fashion has changed somewhat since.

J.N. and in its place we had to buy or we had on charge to us, all this terribly shoddy Ministry of Works furniture. So in the end it was a very good example of false economy.

K.D. Yes.

J.N. I think we got five or six thousand pounds for the stuff that we now would not only – would have appreciated enormously in value and there are still some pieces about that for some reason or another were kept, but we sold a great deal of it.

J.N. Of course, a great deal too was taken away by the Morgan Executors and sent to America, especially the smaller things. There was an absolutely superb wine cellar – legendary wines, which had been kept there – some sherry given by King Alfonso to Pierpont Morgan that had come from.... had 25 years bottle age, which is very rare for sherry. I noticed when the butler took me down there was a crate in the corner full of bottles and I said "What are those? Are they full of ullage or things that have gone wrong?" and he said, "Oh no, that's my personal stock." As indeed, when I went down – part of the terms of the sale were that although we bought everything, the farms and the places, in the arrangement, this particular butler* had to have a cottage at the end of the drive for his lifetime and I once visited him there, for some reason, and found it absolutely stuffed with – well, let's call it Pierpont Morgan furniture, including all – sort of all the ormulu clocks, mainly light, portable articles, and I said, "Good gracious me, you've done yourself well" and he said "All left to

---

* Name Bingley; very portly, typical butler.

me in the Will." I'm afraid I had dark suspicions; and he lasted for a long time. But we were always very jealous of that place because it would have made an ideal place for staff, or for a couple to live in. And then of course, there was the next development. I remember coming back, of getting Otterspool which helped us to – I mean, that was part of the estate, but we didn't get that first, in the first rush, it was only brought into the college after a year or two.* I think those – oh, there was a sad story, it was again in that first room on the right hand side which has doors that open to make it one big room…

K.D. Now the staff room.

J.N. Now the staff room; there was some lovely 18th. century Chinese wallpaper on that, silk wallpaper, and we left it there and thought that would be – would give it great elegance, something which would not normally be in a College, but so many students, and I'm afraid not only students but teachers who came on courses here, added, let's say added to the pictures**…

K.D. Oh dear.

J.N. that in the end we said, this is hopeless, and so before it was absolutely ruined, we had it all taken down and sold, but it was a pity that we had to do that because it was a unique thing, in any college of education in England, to have had that. The garden staff – when Morgan lived there were 37 staff altogether, including I think about 15† in the garden, and we had to reduce the whole thing to a quarter of that even though we had about 120 people living in it. That reminds me of a thing the butler said – I used to ask him about what it had been like in the old days and one or two stories I remember. He said "Mr Morgan kept himself to himself, you know. We never had more than 30 for the weekend." The great big room that for a time we made the dining room and I think was called the library….

K.D. .. and is now the library.

J.N. was originally the Morgan library. We foolishly again, I think,

---

* Otterspool acquired in about a year and Red House also.

** I.N.D. questioned this and thought object of sale was to raise money (only £70. obtained.)

† About 35 in garden; several greenhouses (8?) Flowers and fruit produced for the Park Lane house. Laundry of Park Lane also done in South. Mr. Steward, head gardener, had association with Blenheim. He was given £2,000 per annum for the garden.t12

took away all the book cases from that which were fitted, to make it look as if it was a dining room.

J.N. on the other hand that was one of the features, because there was nowhere else in the building where you could feed 100 people, and if we hadn't had that, we should have had to put up a hut as a hall. This had dignity and height. However, I was told by the butler that Pierpont Morgan used to sit at a little card table in front of that great fire having his supper on his own. He was, I believe, a very lonely old man when he was here. As the butler said, he kept himself to himself, with 40 other people at a weekend, but I think, in between, in this great place, was very little occupied. Another thing is, his bedroom, which was on the north-west corner, had a special little fire escape, because he was terrified of fire apparently, and this was specially built in, so that even if the rest of the place went up, Pierpont Morgan could get out. The rest of the building, much of it, was an absolute death trap for fire. We did what we could but you see basically, although an ancient building in the midlle and probably going back to the 16th. century, it is nearly all bogus, the front's all sort of pseudo-Scots baronial – and so on, but it was only used by Morgan, I think, for about a month a year....

K.D. So I'm told.

J.N. The rest of the time it was empty except for the staff, eating their heads off and keeping the gardens lovely.

K.D. .. and the greenhouses, presumably, superb flowers.

J.N. The other thing, as well as the cellar, was the garage. There were five Rolls Royces, and some of them scarcely used. There was one immense and beautiful Rolls Royce Tourer but again, I thought, couldn't we get hold of these, but we didn't; they were all sold off to prudent people who got – admitted of course, they were all six or seven years old, but they had scarcely been used, and Mr Hart will probably tell you the history of this, he was sort of senior chauffeur. But they glittered; they had been polished all the war and never used at all. Oh, and it's just odd things that come back. I remember – you will see in the Minutes – great excitement about getting the County Council to agree to have the first bus. When one sees the fleets of vehicles now, it's a change. And this was the most awful austere bus which certainly – I remember one of the Committee saying when it came up and he inspected the prototype, he said "Well at least they won't use this for any-

K.D.. Well, that's certainly very much part of the legend.

J.N. Yes. On staff, well, you know, some people came at the beginning and stayed for a very long time – domestic staff – the two people running the catering and the Matron' side, were right from the beginning, and the Vice-Principal was here, wasn't she, right from the beginning.

K.D.. Yes, we still have Miss Margaret Davies.

J.N. Miss Margaret Davies, the art side. There used to be an art studio at Otterspool, that was a sort of art centre – the Florence of the place, we used to call it. I think those are my main sort of memories – in a way came by chance: that if it hadn't been that the estate was wanted for quite another purpose, which five years later wouldn't have been necessary, because the Town Planning Act after the war would have prevented people building on it anyway; that in order to get something back from central government the Education Committee was implored to find a use for it; we found one use which might never have come off but fortunately, fortuitously again, an urgent need for accomodation for training teachers after the war came up and therefore we got it, and having got it and developed it on that basis and got a start.

J.N. It ws ready-made to be part of the national expansion of the teaching profession which was clearly implicit once the 1944 Act – but, you see, this was all decided before the '44 Act was on the Statute Book; all major decisions about this place were made before that. I think that's about all I can think of.

K.D. The farming side was still organised from here for some years, wasn't it?

J.N. Well, yes. The County Council took over the responsibility; the County Land Agent was responsible for administering the farms and the land other than the, I think it was 17 acres, or 37 acres** that went sort of with the house. We used to have arguments, of course, the Education Department with the Land Agent's department, about the use of land, because we obviously wanted

---

* It was used for Field Week visits of considerable distance.
** Current figure.

LONG THATCH · UFFINGTON · FARINGDON · BERKS.
TELEPHONE UFFINGTON 217.

14 July 1967.

Dear Miss Davis

That was a lovely evening on Wednesday & thank you so much for making it possible. It is lovely, too, being now a (very) back number, to receive such a pleasant welcome as you gave me. Whenever I come back to Wall Hall I re-experience some of the severe pangs it cost me to leave it — though I know I was right to go when I did. You probably know the first six or so principals of Emergency Colleges were picked out by the (then) Board of Education and served up on a plate to the LEA's as premises became available: rather

Letter of thanks written by Miss K. Balfern following the retirement of Miss Pearce in 1967

Aerial view of Wall Hall College – April 1978. Photograph taken by Nigel Gates and Hugh Jones, from a height of 1000 feet.
Photograph sent by Miss A.K.Davies.

more and more land –

K.D.. That continues, I think.

J.N ... for the College, but we got 37 acres and the house, I think, for something like £25,000 – it must be the cheapest College of Education, initially ever started in this century, I should think. But it was because of this sequence of events and as I say, it had been a private house, in this century, of one of the richest men in the world, it's been a centre for resistance workers in occupied Europe, and it's been a maternity home and a place to prepare people for the teaching profession – that's all in 30 years.

K.D.. Yes, it's an incredible story, isn't it, fascinating. Well, thank you very much.

CHAPTER 4B

MISS K. M. BALFERN'S MEMORIES

WALL HALL 30 YEARS ON BY MISS K.M.BALFERN

Birth pangs

I first arrived at Wall Hall on a bleak evening in January, 1945, having spent the day at the Belgrave Square offices of the then Board of Education. Since the war was still on, the whole place was blacked out and it seemed ages before the measured tread of Mr Hart was heard in the Hall and the bolts driven back. I had only met Mr Newsom, then the Director of Education for Herts., just a few minutes before we started our journey from London to what was to be the College – handed, so to speak, to him on a plate and introduced to him as the 'Principal' (All the first Principals were appointed as well as the Staff, by the Board.) I don't know who was the most embarrassed by the situation, he or I. It was not, therefore, till the next morning, that the full glory of the battlemented building burst upon me. Meanwhile, the inside was enough. It was bitterly cold. Besides Mr Hart and his wife, who both made me instantly welcome, there was the secretary, Miss Woolf, who had been there for weeks hostessing courses for teachers at weekends and enjoying considerable freedom from work of any kind in between. During the evening, Miss Woolf and I talked about the College we had to prepare and what we had to do – Mr Newsom having departed soon after delivering me.

In the morning there was a conference on site with two H.M.I's, the architect, who presented me with some large scale plans of the College-to-be, and the builder, whose men were busy knocking down walls and filling the air with plaster dust. It was our task to go over the building with the architect to see what he intended to do and then to decide what use could be made of the rooms for classrooms, dormitories, Staff accomodation and the like. "Hall" in the College sense of the word, there was none. I soon discovered an ally in Miss Beaver, H.M.I. whose ideas and mine concurred concerning which rooms were suitable for the Staff and the number of students who could be expected to inhabit the rooms where they were to sleep. By the end of the morning, we had agreed about 98 was the optimum number who could be, with any degree of comfort squeezed in. I did not, on that occasion, see the 'ruined chapel' behind the garages tho' these we visited, since it was planned to turn them into a Lab., nor did I see much else except Otterspool; this lovely house had its share of student and Staff quarters, and I insisted the Art Room was to be there, feeling the setting would be both more congenial and aesthetically satisfying than Wall Hall itself. After this brief visit, I went back to my College post at Bristol to prepare schemes of work and hopefully, a list of books indispensible to a Library – all this in the intervals of carrying on with my own work. I paid two or three more visits to Wall Hall, where I found the work we had agreed to was proceeding very slowly. Early in March, I was released from my post and took up residence at Wall Hall, my arrival coinciding with the last of the Teachers' Courses. Henceforth we were (Miss Woolf and I) to embark in earnest to turn this building, now in an indescribable state of dust and chaos, into a College. We had two months in which to do so. We had seen some of the Pierpont Morgan furniture left, but it was nothing like enough. The Ministry of Works, Supplies Division, had obligingly sent me catalogues of the furniture they had supplied to Munition Workers' and Bevin Boys' Hostels. So now two kindly men arrived to settle with me what I would require – down to the last knife and fork and sheet and pillow slip. You can imagine for yourselves how well this furniture 'Married' with the Pierpont Morgan. The furniture began to arrive in a surprisingly short time and as the houses were still in the builder's hands, there was no place for it but the large 'Hall' intended to be the Dining Room which had been the Baronial quarters of Pierpont Morgan's library, minus of course any books, (except for a few shelves of 'fakes') which we soon piled high and dangerously, with furniture, which required cleaning. Some of the rooms in the house we could not get into at all – they were full of Red Cross and hospital stores – for when the 'doodle-bugs' attacked, Wall Hall had been used as a Maternity Hospital. It took weeks of writing and 'phoning to get them clear. This was one of the worst frustrations. These rooms proved to be small double ones – as I had surmised from the plans and had counted them in the 98 places we were providing.

Meanwhile, Miss Woolf and I were joined by a housekeeper. She, poor woman, was shortly overwhelmed by measles, and went home to have them, forgetting what she had done with a pile of invoices, so that we could not check much of the furniture which still kept on arriving. This added considerably to our worries. We rattled around like peas in a pod, meanwhile interviewing such domestic staff as could be released to us (not many) nor did the Board of Education think in continents in this matter. A day came when the H.M.I's who originally came down, arrived to see how the builder was getting on. His reaction was "another bloody Inspector!" But as a result of this visit, we were given two more weeks in which to get ready for the opening. The Board seemed reluctant to release to me any information about the students we were to receive – 'tho several enterprising ladies called on me, informed me they were coming, asked many questions about their courses and quarters, which I was unable to answer as fully as I, or they, would have wished. With the help of Mr Hart and some of the garden staff we got those smaller rooms furnished. The Ministry of Works sent down some bottles of linseed oil and I could begin, at last, (spending a whole weekend on the job) to get the furniture clean and polished.

Then at last, the dust and noise subsided, the 'baronial' hall was, it seemed miraculously emptied of all the piled furniture, the lost invoices turned up, and the Ministry of Works canteen tables and chairs arrived. Somehow the rooms were all cleaned by our few domestic staff. Then there arrived the Ministry of Works piece de resistance – well over a hundred covered chairs. These had travelled in a coal truck, naked and unashamed. This was during the week before the Teaching Staff were due to come in to prepare themselves for their work. It was the last straw as far as I was concerned, or at least, so I thought at the time. When they heard of our coal-smitten chairs, the Ministry of Works, rising nobly to the occasion, sent down a posse of men, armed with some very strong cleanser (I wondered then, how often before they had had to do this??) – and the chairs came up *almost* as new.

THE STAFF ARRIVED:

One library book did too. As this was invoiced to Exhall, a college due to open just after we were, the book was sent on its lonely way. As no other books were in sight, nor any prospect of even one, I asked Herts. County Library to help us. Generously they did so. The Staff all piled into the van provided for our use and went over to Hertford, returning some hours later, a little the worse for wear after a long journey in a somewhat spring-less van, with boxes and boxes of books. They had saved the situation.

Before I end this story of the turning of Wall Hall into a recognisable College, by the standards of those days, perhaps, I here must relate a terribly tragic event during my first week of residence in March, the horror of which colours all my memories of the early days of the College. Indeed it was nearly the end of any emergency training at Wall Hall at all. Planes were constantly coming over, but that particular morning, one flew over the College, sounding much too close and making an odd sound. I was in my bedroom getting things together for a visit 'on College business', when I felt, rather than saw, it seem to skim the chimney tops and crash into the wood not far from where the main hostel block is now. (It had been towing a glider and the cable had broken before the plane had attained enough height.) There was nothing we could do but ring for ambulances as the plane and all in it ploughed, burning fiercely into the wood. The men in the glider managed to land safely on the by-pass. Had the plane fallen a few minutes earlier, Wall Hall would have received the impact.

THE STAFF

Most of the Staff were gleaned from schools or from organising posts. Miss Chamberlain, the Vice-Principal, was a headmistress in Norfolk. One morning whilst I was still doing two-jobs-in-one at Fishponds, a student came angrily into my room and "Miss Balfern, you have taken for your Staff the best headmistress in Norfolk – and I was going to apply to teach in her school." I condoled and almost apologised. However, my policy, as far as I could carry it out, during those weeks of trying to get the College prepared, was to have members of Staff either singly, or two or three at a time, down to stay at Wall Hall for a night or two, to talk things over and get to know each other. So when the Staff at last assembled, I knew most of them from having met and hammered out policy. Miss Woolf had duplicated some weeks previously copies for each, of syllabuses and timetables. I endeavoured to give each member of Staff a day free of lectures and also each student, for in such a short course, it was for twelve months, later extended to thirteen, I felt Staff and students would require a "free day" in which to read and think.

The course was divided into three parts – to be arranged as it suited the College.

(1) A preliminary course of six weeks, in which the students were 'broken into' study.
(2) School practice of about two months.
(3) Main Course. The students studied a special subject as well as education and courses designed for preparing teachers for Nursery, Infant and Junior Schools. All these courses had been worked out before the Staff met. When we had our first meetings then, there were 'jumping off' points for modifications and discussions. We planned an Environmental Course which, combined Geography, Biology and History, which would, we hoped, give the students an approach to children's work which would be new to them – giving them an entirely new concept of the inter-action of one element of the course on each other. I will say now, that in spite of all the spade work that had been done, the College would hardly have got off the ground if it had not been for the ability and keenness of the Staff, they were all women of ability and determined to make a success of the adventure we were all in together. To their hard work and unremitting effort, the College, in great measure, owed the good reputation it speedily obtained with the Board, the L.E.A. the teachers in the vicinity and later, in the larger educational world.

THE FIRST STUDENTS

Somehow all of the preliminary discussions were over, the Staff each knew what they were to be responsible for, individually and collectively they had latitude in how they interpreted their syllabuses and indeed the courses – the last bed was made, rations for the weekend (only!) were provided and the students arrived. It was a pouring wet day, but no bad weather could dim the lovely daffodils crowding the gardens – nor our enthusiasm. We had acquired at long last, the Board's notes on each individual student on her interview; also about a dozen day students who supposedly lived near enough to come daily. I met them all individually before tea, and afterwards, in the evening, the Staff and I met them together.

They also had a Sunday in which to settle in. The age-range was from twenty-one to forty-eight, most of them were in their early or late thirties. They came, since the War was still on, mainly from civil war-time occupations – factories, War-time Ministries, to Land Army etc. There were one or two only from the forces, having been invalided out. Very few had a full General School Certificate, old style, some had no paper qualifications at all; others had passed in one group of subjects only in the old general schools examinations – often these had failed French and thus the whole examination. No one had to live solely on civilian rations – all had had canteen meals as well. This proved one of our worries. The Board gave us no 'kitty' of supplies, in consequence, we had to supplement our meals, as far as possible, with salad from the garden and bread, (shortly afterwards, bread ad lib. was denied us by the post-war bread rationing.) Thus for the first few months, we were always hungry. Students who went home for weekends were horrified when their loving families provided them with salad as a treat!

We divided the students into three groups for the preliminary course. The infant and nursery groups went straight into School Observation – helped by Staff notes and evening discussions. The junior group, which was from the first, the largest, stayed in College and had a preliminary canter in Art, English and the Environmental work was begun with them. After a fortnight the College changed over. After this the preliminary course continued for another month, all the students having a course in Art, English and Environmental work. I have always regarded, and still do, a course in Art as an important preliminary to a teacher training, under the right teacher. After this the main course began. This went on until the middle of November, with a week's break in August. For this all the students chose a subject for study and the chief education and general courses began. Then all the students went into schools in Watford, St. Albans and Hendon, also Edgeware and Mill Hill. The second half of that first school practice took place in January 1946. Then the practice was examined by a team from the Board.

We marked, and these results were confirmed (or otherwise) by the Inspector. The official marking was Pass or Fail. One or two of the students had withdrawn after the preliminary course and the following weeks; one or two had failed to make the Final School Practice Grade, and so departed. The number of these were very small. Then, from the end of January, with a break at Easter, the Main Course was resumed. At the end of that time, the whole work of the College was examined by a team of H.M.I's. Then thirteen months after we had begun, the first session of students said good bye and a somewhat weary Staff had a holiday of about eight weeks. Then in August the second session began. There were two referred students who came back for a term, and we acquired one from Exhall also for one term. That, in a nutshell, is how the course worked. Everyone was at high pressure, the Staff not least. All the first session students, who had survived, and most did, obtained posts, for they were urgently needed in the schools. They had to continue some form of study for, I think, a year, after which their certificates, already signed by the College, were endorsed by the Board. This pattern of work was, with the modifications of experience, repeated in session two, with again a large percentage of passes, both in school practice and course work. There were some casualties, inevitably, in both sessions, but the quality of the students and their morale, was high, and a lot of very good work indeed was done. One student, at the end of session two, went on to a school of art for an extra term as a reward of merit. This happened similarly in music.

SOME STUDENTS – AND A FEW PROBLEMS.

I should like to tell you about the students of both sessions. But I have only space for a few stories. Session two contained many more ex-service people, who took a short while to settle down to doing jobs for which we asked for volunteers. They were still afraid of 'fatigues'. But in a short time, they too volunteered with a will. That was the main difference at first, between the attitude of the two groups. From the beginning, we had instituted breakfast-in-your-own-room on Sundays. This would, we thought, help students to feel free to rest, to feel at home. In session one, the first senior student – we changed twice a year after the Preliminary Course, had been a professional tap dancer. She was the eldest and a charming person. She was the first Old Student to obtain a Headship. One student in session one ran away after three or four days. Her mother came to see me almost in tears, lest she should 'lose her chance' but she was persuaded to return and made a very good student indeed. Cold feet, I think. The second senior student of session one – a very capable girl – had an accident whilst playing games, and it was feared she had fractured her skull. So she disappeared to hospital, and thence to a relative to recuperate, returning a few days before the end of the session. (I think.) She is now the Head of a nursery school and has received the M.B.E. for the good work she is doing. One student in the second session, the same one who afterwards had the extra term for art, came from the A.T.S. in which she had been a Corporal. I shall always remember her clinging to my door handle after I had greeted her, to say "I have never been *welcomed* anywhere before." It transpired that before the war she had been first a nursery governess, and then had become a 'mother's help living in'. We had several ex-refugees in session two – all of whom had had very sad experiences in their past. I like to think Wall Hall helped them to lead a happy and useful life.

There were some untoward incidents early in the first session. For instance, I had to dismiss the cook for being drunk one fine morning. As a consequence, since new sober cooks are not found very quickly, the Staff and I took it in turns to cook the meals, until Herts. C.C. took mercy on us and sent a meals supervisor to the rescue! Students sometimes interpreted too literally what they had been told, as when a group of nursery students, having had it dinned in to them that they should always be on the look-out for junk, which might prove useful on school practice (and perhaps later) visited the sewerage farm, where one spied a very old saucepan which she thought might be useful for her purposes. So, she picked it up, only to be sternly told "Hi! You can't do that there 'ere Miss!" She had taken the sewerage farm's pet skimmer.

INFLUENCE OF PLACE

Wall Hall itself – the graciously mellow Otterspool House and above all the lovely gardens and grounds, the lanes and countryside around – played a large part in helping students – and Staff – through the hard work. I used to sometimes think the place did as much – almost – as we did for them. Some of the paintings in the art classes particularly showed this. There was one little Jewish girl who came from the East End of London, who'd never seen Spring in the country before. She chose one day to paint a white cherry tree in the hedgerow, it was an exquisitely sensitive piece of work, as rewarding to Miss Davies as to herself.

I cannot end this account of Wall Hall's early days without mentioning a few of the many people who helped us over, sometimes very tall stiles. I hope it has been implicit indeed how constant a support was H.M.I. Miss Beavor and her successor, Miss Price. Nor can I omit the two housekeepers, who in turn, following our first one, who suddenly departed, Miss Prideaux who transformed the housekeeping, and Miss Dickie who followed her, coming from Exhall, and to whom the College owed a great deal. Miss Dickinson, herself, then an Education Officer in Watford, helped to smooth our path in many ways, not least in schools. I was glad to think the College was in her kind and capable hands when I left. Herts. County Council were very good to us, from Mr Newsom, Mr Boyce and Miss Watson to the clerks in the office. Miss Watson it was who represented the county at all the chief domestic appointments. She was a very great help to me.

K. M. BALFERN, 1975.

CHAPTER 4C

TRIBUTES TO MISS K. M. BALFERN

THESE TRIBUTES TO MISS K.M.BALFERN HAVE BEEN CONTRIBUTED BY MEMBERS OF THE OLD STUDENTS' ASSOCIATION AND MEMBERS OF STAFF WHO WERE AT WALL HALL WHEN SHE WAS PRINCIPAL OF THE COLLEGE 1945-1947.

My earliest visits from the Education Office to Wall Hall, in 1945, remain vivid impressions. The first was the Opening by Lord Butler. The spirit of that occasion was of enterprise and determination to fulfil the immediate desperate need for teachers able to bring maturity and inspiration to the post-war schools. On that first day, I remember Kay Balfern's eagerness and down to earth courage in facing the task and the pervading sense of exhilaration.

She was always sincerely concerned with the relationship between the work at the College and the needs of the Schools. I never remembered any friction in arrangements for School Practice, but she knew precisely what she wanted and said so in clear terms.

Kay Balfern was always hospitable, though lack of fuel and food rationing made hospitality extremely tricky. On one occasion her generosity produced a good strong sherry which was greatly enjoyed after a long day's work with little sustenance, but how long and unsure was the trek to the dinner table on the dais at the furthermost end of the Dining Hall! How enjoyable her conversation over a meal consisting, or so it seemed, mainly of beetroot, as it ranged from the deeply educational to the ludicrously hilarious!

Later, on the eve of her departure for Brighton, no-one could have been more helpful in initiating me into the aims and organisation of the College and the foundations laid by her and the Staff made my task immeasurably easier.

K. N. DICKINSON. (SECOND PRINCIPAL)

On looking back it seems to me that one of Kay Balfern's great qualities was her ability to make time to enjoy and share the smaller happinesses and pleasures and the unexpected humours and little dramas of our day to day life at Wall Hall; and all this in a very busy life, lived with an abiding high seriousness of purpose, to which she gave so much of herself in a truly creative thought and energy and determination.

She gave Ben, my corgi puppy, a very warm welcome when I acquired him early in the first year. However, one day, with a sad lack of commonsense, I left him alone in the Staff Room and he passed the time by tearing off and then chewing, part of the fringe from a Pierpont Morgan chesterfield. Kay was away for the day and I spent that evening and much of the night re-making the thing. I had not known her long and was very apprehensive of her re-action to this wanton act of destruction. When next day we went to confess, she listened to the sad story and then chuckled with a rather infectious enjoyment, almost a relish, of the wickedness, ruffled Ben's head and said "Oh, you're a beautiful villain", and thereafter, delighted in any further tales of villainy! On another occasion she looked after him for an evening and on my return presented me with a formal "Progress and Behaviour report".

The first thing for which I always give thanks was her warm and sympathetic understanding of the significance of the work done in the Studio and the sensitive encouragement she gave to it, both in planning for the Studio to be in the lovely setting of Otterspool and in the fact that she saw all the work in relation to the student who had done it and its meaning for her.

MARGARET E. DAVIES. (ART TUTOR)

To those of us who were privileged to be admitted to Wall Hall in its year of conception "Katie" Balfern as Principal was no mere figurehead. We had not come straight from school, we were mature in so far as we had previously earned our living, held responsible posts and a few were even war widows with small children for whom the making of a new life was very necessary. What a challenge for anyone to have to mould us into a new pattern of learning and fit us for our great educational tasks ahead. To this challenge "Katie" rose magnificently – slight in build but what hidden depths and reserves of her strength we were to discover.

Her conscientious attention to detail made her an excellent administrator whilst her enthusiasm and fine analytical mind and always constructive criticism broke down all barriers and endeared her to us all.

What sound advice she gave at the end of our auspicious year which really sped all too soon – "Go forth – never stop learning – always have a receptive mind – be adaptable – face up to every challenge – you are the pioneers." Such was her deep concern for us all and this is the true measure of her loss to education for all.

S.H. SCHOFIELD. (STUDENT)

To Kay Balfern people mattered – not just people in the mass but as individuals. This side of her character revealed itself so clearly from the beginning in her reception of and subsequent dealings with the motley group of mature students which arrived at Wall Hall in May 1945, for we were indeed a motley group in terms of age, background and experience. The venture was new, the first of its kind in this country. It called for a new type of leadership, someone prepared to adapt to different situations and to meet unexpected challenge and many of us can vouch for its results. She had no time for smallmindedness, humbug was quickly seen through as was laziness or inefficiency.

May 1945 was an important point in time for this country; it was also a turning point in the lives of many of us and I venture to believe a landmark in Kay Balfern's own life. It was certainly a time which many of us will remember with gratitude and gladness and with a good deal of humour, for nothing missed the eagle eye of Kay Balfern. She will long be remembered with deep affection by so many of us.

D.M. *nee* P. (STUDENT)

Through the mists of thirty years I can recall Miss Balfern's quiet voice and manner very clearly, as well as her strength of character. As a Staff we all had to be adaptable and found ourselves, before the first students arrived, painting radiators at Otterspool and sweeping up years of dust in the large entrance Hall at Wall Hall, as well as preparing our own lecture rooms and discussing policies with colleagues. When we all met at the end of such a day, K.M.B. loved to hear about amusing incidents – over our rather sparce evening meals of bread, cheese and lettuce. It was a time of strict rationing!

Informality suited K.M.B. I remember, particularly, the Staff meetings on the white seat under the cedars or on the red plush fender in the Staff Common Room. K.M.B. liked people – from the many official visitors, to the children who came to see the exciting Nursery exhibitions – from 'Rab.' Butler when he opened the College a year after his 1944 Education Act, to the small visitor whom she encouraged to water the estate with his toy watering can.

She was highly thought of in wider Educational fields. Once when I took her place on a Selection Board in Chelmsford I was asked why my "Grande Dame" had not come and during the meeting I realised how much they missed her shrewd and apt contributions to the discussion.

H.G. (TUTOR)

I have one very light hearted recollection of her keen sense of humour. Some four or five of us had been to a local dance; on our return we had to report to the person on duty. We were only in the nick of time and rather high spirited, but she greeted us with a twinkle in her eye. The next morning at Assembly the hymn announced was "Dear Lord and Father of mankind, forgive our foolish ways." You can imagine the ripple of amusement amongst the revellers of the night before.

M.S. *nee* C. (STUDENT)

CHAPTER 4D

TRIBUTES TO MISS N. DICKINSON

TRIBUTES TO MISS NANCY DICKINSON PRINCIPAL OF WALL HALL COLLEGE FROM 1947–65/6

Miss Dickinson's two Godsons and her niece Mary arranged and spoke at the service. This is what Jonathon Dickinson said: (kindly sent to the Association by Mary Dickinson)

Although we are here to mourn Nancy's death, it is of course her life that really matters. We can be thankful that she did have so many activities and worthwhile years and that during those years she had so many friends who loved and respected her. So now is also the time to take pleasure in all your good memories of her and be glad that you were able to share your lives with her.

Nancy was born in Birmingham, the eldest of four children. Her father was the Headmaster of Halesowen Grammar School, where Nancy herself received a very good education. A feature of this school was that it was the first co-educational grammar school in the country. Nancy was particularly good at French, so on leaving school she continued her French studies at Bedford College, part of London University. After completing her degree course, she was appointed French teacher at a school in Ipswich, her first job in a long career in education. It was at this school that she met her life-long friend Eileen.

When her father died, Nancy returned to Birmingham and taught at King Edward's High School for Girls. Then, in 1936 she came south again and became one of the first teachers at the newly built Copthall Girls' School at Mill Hill near London. Nancy started her involvement in education management and training when she moved to the Hertfordshire Education Department at Watford in 1943. This led, in 1947, to her helping to establish the Wall Hall Teacher Training College at Aldenham, of which she became the

Principal. This was the culmination of her career and she was very highly regarded by everyone who knew her. She remained in this appointment until her retirement in 1965/66.

Nancy was an ideal choice for the job. In addition to her teaching abilities she had all the social skills and graces needed to lead such a college and inspire respect and loyalty both from the staff and students. As a result she made many friends from all over the world and many people are to this day grateful for what she gave them.

After her retirement she bought a flat in Watford Heath and started being active in many other ways. Almost immediately she spent ten months going round the world, lecturing and visiting ex-students and friends in many countries. She took up Bridge and developed a keen interest in the game; she became an active member of the W.I. and National Trust and went to art appreciation classes. She enjoyed going to concerts and took part in plays put on by the local amateur dramatic society.

In the mid-1970's Nancy moved to Little Chalfont where she continued with these activities. She also acquired a garden which she enjoyed looking after, often with the help of Mary with whom she was the best of friends. Some years ago they visited Egypt and India together.

Nancy was very much a lady of her era; controlled, well organised and invariably polite and pleasant to everybody. She always saw the best in other people and tried to see the other person's point of view, even if she did not agree with it. She had a remarkable knack of retaining friendships right until the end of her life. This year for example, she sent and received over 100 Christmas cards from all over the world. There are clearly going to be many people who will now miss her very much, while remembering her with gratitude and a lot of love.

From Miss A. K. Davies – Nancy Dickinson was loved and respected. I knew her only after her retirement when I succeeded her as Principal of Wall Hall College, as it then was.

Her imagination and resourcefulness was very apparent in the college; in the design and lay out of new buildings, in the creation of the open air theatre and the swimming pool to name but a few examples. She managed the college with much skill and gave it a particular expertise in the training of mature students.

Being a small college it was possible to have something of the family atmosphere which large institutions cannot replicate. Nancy gave me much help and support. I was particularly grateful for her generous loan of her flat while she toured the world. Many others will have memories of her kindnesses. She gave a great deal to Wall Hall and maintained a close interest in its changing affairs and the people associated with the college. Nancy enjoyed people and social activities and was a superb hostess and loved organizing a party.

The last years were so difficult for her but she faced them most gallantly. I admired her enterprise and courage in the early days of her disabilities, when she would not let encroaching blindness and deafness prevent her travelling here and abroad, seeing and entertaining her many friends. She took into her room at the Nursing Home her sense of good etaste and style and enjoyed the company of other residents and her own regular walks in the garden. Visitors were, as always, warmly welcomed. As one of her old students said to me on hearing of her death "She was a remarkable woman and splendid person." She will be warmly remembered.

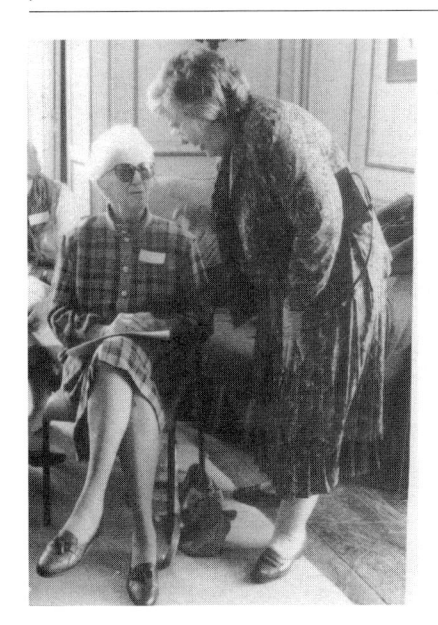

Miss Nancy Dickinson (seated) speaking to Miss A. K. Davies in 1993. This was the last time Miss Dickinson was able to attend Wall Hall.

From Margaret Smeaton – It is sad to think that in her latter years disabilities prevented her from enjoying life to the full. She gave me the opportunity to enjoy teaching at Wall Hall and I shall long remember the Christmas parties of which she was the life and soul. She stayed with us several times after she retired. A delightful guest, who was always interested in what was going on around her.

"Are you going down to the new Geography Department? Don't. The builders have put a six inch nail through the electric cabling and you will not be able to move in until they have repaired it." She had climbed the stairs to the staff flat in South to deliver the latter message. The original building expansion was fraught with difficulties but Nancy took more than a passing interest in what the builders were doing and alleviating the frustration of one geography lecturer who had to organise the moving of equipment from the old dairy. Other recollections from those days of a college expanding in student numbers to counteract the teacher shortage are the second years' effort at the Christmas entertainment – a parody on the current hit "Fings ain't wot they used to be!" Nancy

A photograph showing Miss M. E. Davies (Art Tutor) with her dog on her knees. Note the conservatory with its decorative top and also the greenhouses visible through the glass to the right of the picture. 1946–47.

enjoyed that as she enjoyed most parties. I cannot forget the number of hats which were produced by Win Pearce and herself to be distributed to those members of staff who had been so careless as to turn up to a Christmas fancy dress party without one. Academically one was allowed to organise a department's work as one thought appropriate though Nancy ensured that it fitted in with her ideas of the needs of the future primary school teachers. She appreciated the need for a broad curriculum and Special Feature Days were her device for breaking down what shebreaking down what she to be the rigid subject teaching in secondary schools alien to the way in which young children learned.

College Engagements, varying from poetry readings by John Laurie and the Barrow Poets to a talk on prison life and reforms from Duncan Fairburn and music recitals, widened horizons.

I knew Wall Hall at the beginning of the times of expansion from a College providing a three year certificate for about 120 students to one which eventually grew to an institution for several hundred awarding degrees. It was Nancy who laid the foundations for this. There must be many generations of teachers who, reviewing their time at Wall Hall look back with appreciation to the ethos which she created which not only stood them in good stead professionally, but also created a college which, perhaps not as well known as some, had a national reputation of quiet renown.

From Dr. John Hunter – My first meeting with Miss Dickinson was during the spring of 1963 and so that is getting on for 40 years ago… a long time I'm afraid, but it was an occasion I am unlikely to forget. Having applied to Wall Hall for a post in the Education Department, I was delighted to receive an offer of an interview and this turned out to be an 'interesting' occasion to say the least! The first person to interview me was the Vice Principal, the seemingly very formidable Miss Pearce and then before lunch I was introduced to the Principal, Miss Dickinson who appeared to me to be every bit as regal as the Queen herself with not a hair out of place and dressed to perfection! If Miss Pearce had tested me on my knowledge of the classroom, I think Miss Dickinson had other tests in mind. For example, I recall being offered sherry already poured out on a silver tray... sweet sherry and dry sherry. Fortunately I don't like sweet sherry, so I probably passed that test if it was part of the 'test'! Then came the walk downstairs from her office at the top of the mansion to the dining room... and I did hold the doors open for... and yes, I did use my cutlery correctly... and yes, I did talk to the Heads of Department sitting at the same table... and no, I didn't slurp my soup!! However, in spite of all, I was not offered the post in the Education Department but a post for which I had not applied, half time geography and half time History. I gladly accepted and never regretted it for one moment. I believe we did a good job at the college preparing our students for the rough and tumble of the classroom but good manners, good appearance and good standards of behaviour also mattered in the way Miss Dickinson ran the college and in her very high expectations of both staff and students both personally and professionally. The formidable Miss Pearce turned out to be, as I thought, formidable but a lady full of fun and our Christmas staff parties were wonderful occasions while Miss Dickinson remained regal, charming, amusing and the sort of person for whom a latter day Sir Walter Raleigh would gladly have laid down his cloak. Eventually I did get a post in the Education department and became its Head before moving on to become Principal of Gloucestershire College of Education after 10 very happy years at Wall Hall. Certainly as Principal, I never forgot the lessons learned from Miss Dickinson and from her successor Miss A. K. Davies.

From Dr. Haslam – My first meeting with Nancy was in 1959 when, as the husband of one of her students, I attended the College Formal Ball. Nancy presided over the occasion with a relaxed and friendly formality, supported by her residential colleagues. She took an obvious pleasure in her conversations with students and their guests.

It was five years later that I was appointed to the academic staff of Wall Hall. Although it was to be Nancy's final year as Principal, it was stimulating for a young lecturer to observe her dedication to the college, a commitment which was shared by staff and students.

This was the beginning of a period of expansion of the college, with rapidly increasing members of staff and students and a substantial building programme. Although this must have placed a heavy work load on Nancy she continued to be available to staff and students and to enjoy the social occasions of the college. Her previous experience as a Divisional Education Officer in Hertfordshire had enabled her to establish excellent working relationships with senior officers at County Hall and with members of the Education Committee which smoothed the period of transition. Having a familiarity with architectural procedures and plans, she took a particular interest in the details of the building programme.

On her retirement, Nancy made a leaving gift to the college of a most generous contribution towards the cost of an open-air swimming pool which has since been enjoyed by generations of students and staff and their families and friends.

Nancy maintained a close interest in the college during her retirement and continued the friendships she had established there. She visited the Wall Hall Association at its Annual General Meetings and attended many formal events at the college. Her loss will be mourned by all who knew her.

From Joan Hill (McKay) – My first memories of Nancy Dickinson are of a gracious lady whose friendly welcome to the Staff and whose encouragement to experiment and to adapt to the demands of a college syllabus, yet keeping sight of the children, meant much. Then events moved quickly from 1960 onwards – the three year certificate and the two year mature students' certificate were established. Then, there was a move to increase the emphasis of the academic quality of the course, but to retain the needs of the children.

News came that numbers would grow, so plans were made for a gym, five new hostels, a sick bay and staff residence, a science block and adaptation of existing premises for other purposes.

To both the academic side and the environmental side, Nancy gave of her skills and knowledge and so helped to create a firm basis for more expansion and the changes in education and society in years to come. She was concerned for everyone's achievement and for a pleasant environment in which all could work, hence her concern to save a wisteria from the "axe". It decorated a wall of the gym.

Her love of the theatre was great and she was always game for a theatre visit. This love was reflected in her support for drama in the outdoor theatre in the varied facilities of college. She enjoyed an unexpected and quick tease of one and social activities be they in college or on a visit to a college in Ranum, Denmark. It was appropriate that she retired at Christmas so that not only the usual festivities but a happy champagne popping Wild West Show gave her a happy send-off on a world tour which would include a visit to one time Malayan students of the college. She returned to enjoy friends and playing bridge, among other interests.

At a personal level Miss Dickinson saw the best in everyone. In all the years I knew her I never heard her say a word against anyone. Her attitude was always positive. She was readily approachable, sympathetic, supportive and encouraging. Efforts made in the course of work were quickly noted and her appreciation registered. There was never any doubt as to who was the leader. She gave her energy unstintingly to the college, to which her interest and loyalty remained throughout her long life. She was an icon of her time.

From Nan Hill – We were saddened to hear of Nancy's death. It was devastating to see such deterioration in one of her calibre who had been such an inspiration throughout her working life. Her contribution to the college was enormous – unstinting and generous at all times. Later, too, we continued to value her friendship and have missed her for some time.

It must be with a sense of relief to all that she has been released from such a poor quality of life in the end.

From Noel Minnis – She was a marvellous person and a marvellous Principal of Wall Hall. She combined a wealth of skills as an administrator with such a wise regard for truly liberal education which inspired staff and students alike. I have always felt deeply indebted to her for introducing me into teacher training with such wide guidance. But above all she had a wonderful gift of making friends being so understanding and generous in all personal relationships.

She had a great sense of occasion too and if she was well enough, to appreciate the advent of the new millenium must have gladdened her greatly.

From Mary Fernandez Morris – I shall remember her as a remarkable woman with a brilliant mind, a spur to all who worked with her. Knowledgeable of all, always up to date, involved with everything yet always having the time and interest to concern herself with us all, a concern which continued to the last.

Nancy interviewed me for my post in 1962, a day I have never forgotten. We had a splendid hour or so, mostly talking about architecture and life… not at all about C.V's or even teaching. She gave me the job. I hope I repaid her trust. I was at Wall Hall for twenty years.

From Sue Baggin – She was a wonderful character who touched so many people's lives. Her life though is surely one to celebrate as she achieved so much and lived her life to the full. I remember her with great affection.

From Nell Attwood – Those of us who were fortunate enough to have known her through Wall Hall will sense the end of an era. People who attended the annual re-unions very much looked forward to meeting up with Nancy each year, even though many of them were not at the College in her day. Such was the respect for her. Even in later years and with failing eyesight, she would make the rounds of each table after lunch. She made people feel she was really interested in when they were at College and in what they subsequently achieved. I remember particularly the year she celebrated her 90th. birthday and on receiving a gift from the Association, she stood up and talked for ten minutes or more. It was interesting and very funny and her recall of the early Wall Hall times were amazing – all without a single note.

I hope if I get to that age I might even look half as good as Nancy at 90. What a great looking lady she was and always so beautifully groomed. She will be missed and lovingly remembered.

From Vivienne Perkins- Many of us can bear witness to the unique sense of community she created as Principal of Wall Hall. For her every individual was special.

From a colleague at the Divisional Education Office- Nancy and I started working together in a cramped room in the Watford Town Hall in (I think) 1945 representing the newly established Divisional Education Office for South West Hertfordshire – probably one of the first to be established under the Butler Education Act. We were immediately required to draw up development plans for dozens of new schools, blueprints for catchment areas, reorganise secondary education, organise and service a network of new committees and governing bodies. Little did we know what we had let ourselves in for! We became cross-eyed with calculations and drafts. But, funnily enough I don't think we went far wrong.

By a strange co-incidence, Jean Davidson, the Headmistress of Watford Girls' Grammar School and Dorothy McHugh, the Headmistress of Chorleywood College for Blind Girls, were both former colleagues and good friends of Nancy which helped to integrate us into the local education service.

I remember when the Pierpoint Morgan Estate was sold and staff were allowed after the main sale, to buy any "left-overs" which we both did, little guessing that this would become Nancy's home. From the Watford Town Hall we moved to Little Cassiobury, a charming and elegant 18th. century house in the grounds of the new Technical College and scheduled for demolition as part of the College development. We were able to prevent this and save the house for use as the headquarters of the Divisional Education Offices which we both loved and found it a delightful place in which to work.

County Hall eventually responded to our plea for transport by giving us an old, very basic delivery van discarded by the Schools' Meals Service. It caused much merriment as we drove up to schools and meetings, but we became quite attached to it!

I don't think Nancy and I ever had a cross word, we didn't always agree, but we were able to work things out. Unfortunately, people would sometimes wish to see me, or refer something to me, even though Nancy clearly had the better knowledge and experience, because I was a man and she was only a woman. Those were still the sexist days! But Nancy won through on this issue. We were both sad when she was appointed to Wall Hall and our partnership ended, but our friendship endured.

From Gwen Batham – Whilst chatting with her I learnt that Nancy grew up in the village of Halesowen, at the bottom of Mucklow's Hill, a cycle ride from Quinton, Birmingham, at the top of the Scarp, where I grew up. When I was young there were many small villages, some just inside the industrial 'black country' all of which are engulfed by the sprawling mass of Greater Birmingham. There are still a few open spaces surrounding the Clent Hills which we'd explored as children. Both Nancy and I remembered the bluebells in Franklin which carpeted the woods – now unfortunately no more, being buried under the Service Station and the M5 motorway! Perhaps that is why we both loved those in Wall Hall grounds, as they reminded us of happy childhood days. She was surprised to learn that some of my family still live in Halesowen and that there is now a wide by-pass. I used this frequently to visit Kinver, where my parents moved to on retirement. She also knew Kinver and said how nice it was to chat to someone who knew the area as it was and is now!

From Valerie Canton – She remained independent as long as she could in spite of her failing sight and hearing, plus she had a pacemaker. When she could no longer drive, she continued to play bridge and read large print books. She had a stair lift installed. At Wall Hall, during her last couple of visits, she found it difficult to hear with all of the background noise. She had devices so she could hear on the phone, but it was difficult for her to communicate with the other patients, which caused her to become isolated. However, she did keep in touch with lots of people and last Christmas she sent and received more than a hundred cards!

From Joan Beagle – Miss Dickinson had a genuine love for young people and wanted to help them to attain their full potential. She interviewed me when I was applying to Wall Hall to do a two-year mature course. She soon put me at my ease and began gently probing into my background and qualifications – almost as if we were two old friends catching up with the latest news. She advised me to do the three year course instead, as it would give me more time to fit in my family commitments. So, I did the three year course and thoroughly enjoyed it. It was good advice. She was practical as well as imaginative. She had that priceless ability to put people at ease. She seems to have gone on helping young people after she had retired and to have had a full and interesting life.

My colleagues and I were lucky we were at Wall Hall at the same time with her as such a very special person. Goodbye to a friend.

CHAPTER 4E

STUDENTS IN 1946 AND 1950

THE EARLY YEARS AT WALL HALL
BY AN OLD STUDENT OF 1946.

One can look back on one's life and always reminisce on some of the happenings that have been more than landmarks but what have been a complete turning point – a time one remembers with great happiness or the reverse!

I was one of the first of the Emergency Trained, being in the second year; I had left school over twenty years previously. The great call after the war, was for teachers with a capital T. Was this what I was being called to do? – to give up what was considered a 'safe' job with a pension etc.? I took the plunge and now look back with pride and pleasure that I was ever considered and given the opportunity to serve the education world in this way. Arriving at Wall Hall early in August, 1946, with fear and trepidation, not quite knowing why I had made this 'mad move', I was soon to face the Principal – was I scared! (but she soon became a good friend to me.)

Then the dormitory accommodation, the first meal, the first lecture, an essay to write, all so strange, but being only 100+ students and all to face a six week general course we soon found that we were like a large family. We had come from all walks of life – the Army – A.T.S., the Navy – W.R.E.N., the Air Force – W.R.A.F., and the Land Army etc., etc. The first greatest thrill for me was the beauty of the surroundings with so many varieties of trees and the vast and beautiful grounds, the peach houses, the grape vines, Otterspool etc., I had always lived in a busy London street.

The meals were served in what had been the Library – the shelves now cleared of books, but soon to take our little pots of rations – 3ozs. butter; 4ozs. margarine and 4ozs. sugar, all to last a week – bread was also rationed as were cakes (were there any?) So every meal was quite a feast.

Physical Education – yes, some very stiff bodies and aching limbs – no such thing as a Gym. – so we performed in the entrance Hall! The winter was one of the worst on record 1946/47, and on rare occasions we were sent out to run in the snow, to get our frozen limbs more frozen – we were only allowed one bar electric fires in our study rooms and there were power-cuts too! So, we wrapped ourselves in blankets to study.

Yes, at times it was grim, but the enthusiasm was prominent and nothing stopped us putting our all, into our work. We had to pack the whole course into thirteen months with three school practices and only very short holidays, so we often worked into the night, but I look back on it as some of the happiest days of my life. We had our times of fun and laughter and made such friends, many of whom, like myself are retired and we look forward so much to the yearly reunion and meeting again for the holiday we spend together for a painting course, which has now become a yearly event inspired by Miss Margaret Davies. (No name available.)

The Red House originally built to house Land Army girls 1939–1945, and sold in the 1990s as a private residence

RECOLLECTIONS OF WALL HALL TEACHER'S TRAINING COLLEGE – 1951/1952

It was on Saturday, 23rd. September 1950 when I and fifty plus other girls gathered in the Common Room – to the right of the main entrance – to be welcomed to Wall Hall Teachers' Training College by quietly spoken Miss Dickinson the Principal, Miss Pearce the Vice-Principal and a handful of other tutors, all, needless to say, female. Among them I remember, motherly Miss Jones, round and bouncy Miss Bailey, Miss Gooderson, Miss Firth and Miss Fairweather. We were the first group of students to be admitted to do the statutory two year course and most had come straight from school. There were still a few older students about the College completing their emergency training course of one year, but they left in the spring of 1951.

In those days we took very little with us to college, our clothes, a few personal belongings, some text books and our bicycles – none of the paraphernalia that students of two or three decades later considered to be essential. Our bikes were needed for getting speedily from one site to another.

Accommodation was on three sites, about half the girls had rooms in the main building, the remainder were divided between Otterspool, an old lodge or possibly coaching inn (haunted, I understand) down the drive to the west of the main building, and Red House, a large modern house in the village. There was also accommodation at Holbrook, above a science room. This was a recently constructed building immediately next to the estate farm, a working farm with livestock, cows, pigs and horses.

The majority of us shared rooms with one or two other girls. I was at Red House sharing a room with Thelma. There were two other rooms shared by two girls, two rooms shared by three and a single room which I was lucky enough to have in my second year. One tutor lived here with us – Miss Jones – a lovely lady who retired at the end of our first year.

Rooms were sparsely furnished. For each girl there was a bed, a chest of drawers, a narrow wardrobe plus a small, square table and hard straight-backed chair. There was no central heating, so each room had a small electric fire. (How did we keep warm in those days, when winters were colder than they are now! I remember the very thick snow in December 1950.) Clean bedlinen came in a large laundry basket, I do mean a basket, not a plastic thing, every Thursday. We put our dirty sheets etc. in it on Friday mornings.

There were few house rules, we could only bath twice a week; we had a rota and my days were Tuesday and Friday of each week. Water was heated by a small domestic boiler in the kitchen and we were supposed to keep this stoked with coke, if we didn't, it went out and we had no hot water! I remember that if the wind was in a particular direction, it just wouldn't stay in!

Another rule that applied to all of the girls was that we had to in by 10p.m. each night. If we wanted to be out later than that we had to 'sign out' in a book kept on a table near the front door but, officially, we were only allowed this privilege three times in any one term. However, I believe the last bus from Watford reached the village just before 10 p.m. so it was unlikely that you'd be any later. There was a telephone in the cupboard under the stairs, but we were only expected to use it in an emergency.

We lived in a very civilized way. All of the meals were taken together in the dining room at Wall Hall, formerly the library of the house, with the staff sitting at the far end. This included breakfast at 8 a.m. so those of us at Red House or Otterspool had a quick cycle ride each morning – (exercise before breakfast you could say!) Lunch was at 1 p.m. and the evening meal at 6 p.m. (These times varied slightly when we were on school practice.) We nearly always sat at the same table, so it was easy for staff checking on us, to see who skipped a meal. Grace was said by Miss Dickinson or another staff member. Many foods were still rationed so ration books were handed over at the beginning of the year, thankfully our sweet coupons were given back to us! We had to have two suitable containers, named, for a weekly allowance of butter and sugar. These were kept in the dining room on top of two sideboards and I cannot remember any of these going missing, as would inevitably happen today.

Lectures usually began at 9.30 a.m. and continued right through the day until 5 p.m. Monday to Friday. We were training to teach primary school aged children, including nursery, so we were divided into groups depending on which stage of primary education we were most interested in. There was a nursery group; two infant groups and a junior group. I was in the nursery group. We concentrated on children aged from two to seven years, but we all covered early child development as well. I remember that one of our text books was called *The Mothering of Young Children*, but it soon became known as *The Smothering of Young Children* by our group. The previously mentioned Miss Bailey was our main tutor, very bright and cheerful and not your archetypal college lecturer.

We had no purpose built lecture halls, but made use of the rooms in the house. The nursery group's tutorial room was in the east wing of the house, there was just enough room for the thirteen of us. A room in Otterspool was used for our; a bright room with views down to the River Colne, and craft activities pottery and needlework took place in, of all places, the old greenhouses, unbearably hot in summer, extremely cold in winter.

The main subjects studied by all groups were the Principles and Practice of Education which included some Psychology and the History of Education, Health Education, Physical Education and English Language. We all did one special subject which was for our own development and could choose from English Literature, History, Geography, Biology, Art, Craft or Music, quite a range for such a small number of students. I chose Geography which had been my strongest subject at school and enjoyed several Field Trips, particularly one to Seaford in Sussex, where we spent several days tramping over the Seven Sisters Cliffs in pouring rain.

We had three periods of school practice during our training, two of three weeks each and the final one of four weeks. I spent the first and third ones in nursery schools, the second in an infants' school, all in Watford. We were very closely supervised and had to submit very detailed lesson plans to the tutors. We had individual meetings with our tutors to discuss any problems we had. School practices were a very stressful time for all of us – up early, a long day in school and evening tutorials. I guess more tears were shed during those times than any other, however, we all passed our final practice and our examinations for the Cambridge Certificate of Education. In addition to the teaching staff, there was a housekeeper in charge of the domestic side of the college. She had a small staff of girls, who also lived in. Then there was Matron, an awesome figure! You went to Matron if you were unwell and she would prescribe an aspirin or two or arrange for you to see a Doctor. I only went to her once, with stomach pains and ended up in Watford Hospital with peritonitis and having to have my appendix removed.

Although we were always being reminded of the intensity of our course, there was a lighter side to life at Wall Hall in the early Fifties. We had group trips to London theatres, summer garden parties in the college gardens with activities such as clock golf, croquet, country dancing and the end of term dances to which young men from a nearby male-only training college were invited. I didn't go to these as I couldn't afford suitable dresses; also, I had already got a boy friend so wasn't particularly interested in meeting other young men. In July 1951, we were hosts to a group of educationalists, college lecturers and headteachers from the far east, Singapore, Malaya and Hong-Kong. I believe they were here to observe teacher training in Britain, but it was quite an event for them and for us, only six years after the War. I made friends with a Miss Seow and, as I lived

An Autumn morning, showing frost on the grass in front of the old Dining Room/Library/Lecture Room.

1802, coloured steel engraving 'View of Otter's pool, near Watford, Herts'

Wall Hall Stable Clock and the Waterlily Pond.

The pavilion in the Italian Garden – after the statue had been stolen.

Looking through the walkway gate towards the Stable Clock, past where some of the old greenhouses were situated by the walk.

The pool in the Italian Garden.

The heated swimming pool used for education and pleasure.

The swimming pool.

The colourful facade of Wall Hall Mansion, which will be fondly remembered by all of the many people who taught, worked and studied there for so many years.

only a few miles from Aldenham, I took her home for a day to meet my family. I kept in touch with her for a few years afterwards.

In September 1951 we were joined by a second group of girls beginning their two year course. Now, some of the two-bed rooms became three and the three-bedded rooms four, but we were still a college of only just over 100 students.

These are my personal memories of Wall Hall in the years I was there, if anything is incorrect, I apologise. There are still many things I could have included, but enough is enough. I would just like to say how lucky we were to be in such tranquil surroundings, a stately home, well kept gardens, lovely views down to the River Colne and green fields with cows quietly grazing. Soon though, there would be a motorway close by, a golf course, and, inevitably, blocks of student accommodation. Ah well. That's progress.

JOAN V. WING July 2002.

CHAPTER 5

PRINCIPALS AND DEANS OF WALL HALL

PRINCIPALS AND DEANS
WALL HALL TEACHER TRAINING COLLEGE 1945
HERTFORDSHIRE COLLEGE OF
HIGHER EDUCATION 1975
WATFORD CAMPUS,
HERTFORDSHIRE UNIVERSITY 1992.

PRINCIPAL	Kathleen Mary Balfern	1945–1947
PRINCIPAL	Nancy Dickinson	1947–1966
PRINCIPAL	Kay Davies	1966–1981
PRINCIPAL	Dr. Derek Haslam	1981–1988
DEAN	Dr. Richard Wheeler	1988–1992
DEAN	Professor Graham Holderness	1992–2003

In 1947 the Principal Miss K. Balfern was appointed to head the Brighton Teacher Training College (later incorporated into the University of Sussex.) Her successor, Miss I. N. Dickinson as Education Officer in the Division, had been involved in the establishment of Wall Hall College and was able to take the College forward, overseeing new courses and new buildings. Her retirement at the end of 1965 was followed by the appointment of Miss A. K. Davies as Principal until 1981, a period of more buildings, new courses, merger with Balls Park College and considerable expansion of numbers. Dr. D. Haslam saw the move to closer ties with the Hatfield Polytechnic and the last Principal Dr. R. Wheeler saw through the absorption of Wall Hall into the new University of Hertfordshire and was himself Dean of Humanities and Education sited at Wall Hall.

A great deal happened in these years and here we can only give snapshots of events, drawing on a variety of records, including the

The Mansion of Wall Hall College of Education.

Newsletters of the Old Students' Association. The illustrations indicate the growing links with other parts of the world as in the course for teachers from Malaysia, and secondments of students to and from the U.S.A. The College continued to recruit large groups of mature students with, in some cases, shortened courses. There was a strong tradition of Field Work relating to practically every subject area, sometimes involving stays abroad. So strong was this tradition in the fields of Science and Geography and the pioneer Bio-Geography course led by their tutor Miss J. Stampe and Miss M. Smeaton, a field group from former students was formed and continues to flourish, organising a very varied programme of visits and supported by a wider membership.

CHAPTER 6.

OFFICIAL OPENING OF WALL HALL

(Re-typed from an article printed in the *West Herts. & Watford Observer* – 18th.May, 1945.)

Set amid most beautiful surroundings, Wall Hall, Aldenham, one time residence of the late Mr Pierpont Morgan, was formally opened on Tuesday as a Teacher's Training College with accomodation for 100 women.

The opening ceremony was performed by the Minister of Education, Mr R. A. Butler, who spoke in glowing terms of the work done by the Hertfordshire Education Committee.

Wall Hall was purchased by the Herts. County Council some months ago, the purchase price being £226,000. Actually the students, 91 of them, took up residence last week. Their ages range from 20 to 40. They have been carefully selected for the course, which will last 12 months. On completing their training they will be drafted to nursery, primary and junior schools.

Presiding, Alderman H. H. Williams (chairman to the County Education Committee) introduced Mr R. A. Butler. They had all admired the manner in which the Minister had shepherded through the House of Commons the new Education Act, he said.

Declaring the college open, Mr Butler said that he was most grateful to the Hertfordshire County Council and Education Committee for the initiative they had shown. That was the first Emergency Training College to be opened and in that respect it signified the beginning of the operation of the Education Act. It was gratifying that Hertfordshire should take the lead, and if he had anything to do with it, he would put more on their shoulders.

The Minister said that there were 18 Boards at work in the country interviewing candidates. There were 8,000 applicants to date, but not all of these would be selected. There was every intention to

The Opening Ceremony Wall Hall Womens' Emergency Teacher Training College in May 1945 by Mr. R. A. Butler

retain the high standard of the teaching profession and they did not intend to take anyone they could get. For that reason he congratulated the students at Wall Hall on surviving the first hurdle.

Many of the young women came from the Civil Defence services or from industry. As yet, they had not begun to deal with the rush that would result from the demobilisation of the Forces, nor would they be dealing with men.

Mr Butler said that it was a mistaken idea that education was some sort of secluded watertight department. It was not intended that there should be no mixing between those at men's and women's colleges. On the success of their worldliness, as well as on their wisdom, would depend the success of their training they would give to the young people under their care.

The teaching profession, said Mr Butler, offered a wide range of opportunity. There would be nursery, primary and secondary education, in different branches, and they might wish to go on to work with young people. The teaching profession of the future would have a wide variety of interest as in any other profession.

Humerously commenting on the "trouble" he got into over the new Burnham scale of salaries, Mr Butler said he was glad that the profession could now offer a reward a little more consistant with its dignity.

Saying that much remained to be done to get up to the 1939 level, Mr Butler said he had been shown at Watford much that was satisfactory. If he had no imagination he could have rested assured that all was well, but he knew there were many schools that he was not shown that were not satisfactory. "I was shepherded by schools at which, had I been driving alone, I might have stopped," said the Minister, amid laughter.

A vote of thanks to Mr Butler was moved by Miss K. Balfern (principal) and seconded by senior student Miss Pennhale.

What was the first Women's Emergency Training College for teachers under the new Education Act, was opened at Wall Hall, Aldenham, on Tuesday, by the Minister of Education. MrButler praised the initiative of the Herts. County Council in the lead given in preparation for the full implementation of the provisions of the Act.

When the estate of the late Mr J. Pierpont Morgan was for disposal, the County Council wisely obtained an option to purchase the mansion and adjoining land. The foresight thus shown has been abundantly justified by subsequent events.

Raising of the school leaving age and smaller classes, as well as extended curriculum, demand more teachers, and Wall Hall supplies the first attempt to give a one year intensive training to women teachers, of whom 100 can be accomodated. They come from the various walks of life and ages range from 20 to 40. Thoroughly trained teachers, modern and well equipped schools, and the ever present aim of education for life, rather than merely for vocation, are indispensable requisites for bringing to full fruition all the possibilities envisaged in the new Measure.

A pre-view of the new education scheme has been offered in Watford by the Education Week which concludes today. The Minister found time to visit two of the exhibitions on Tuesday, by which he saw something of the high standard of the present work and the potentiality of the new technical college in specialised training for the area's manifold industries.

A photograph of people gathering in front of the Mansion after the Opening Ceremony

CHAPTER 7

THE MALAYSIAN TEACHERS 1951

OVERSEAS TEACHERS' COURSE AT WALL HALL TRAINING COLLEGE – 1951

Miss Dickinson spoke to the Students at the end of their stay in England, stating the aim of their visit was to explain the English way of living and English education. This was done not with lectures alone, but with a diverse provision for education, working and leisure time development. The Students were shown as fully and honestly as possible, the way English people live and how they try to educate their children.

Visits were arranged to study a variety of villages, market towns and industrial towns – to see London with its sprawling new outskirts, its slums and rehousing schemes, its patchwork of wealthier areas and its historic monuments; to see the sort of social and economic conditions which brought about the pattern of English education with its merits and its problem of overcrowded schools, large classes and shortage of teachers.

Miss Dickinson said it was important to remember that we now have to provide free full time education for every one of the six million English children between the ages of five to fifteen and for the continued education from fifteen to eighteen, of at least a proportion who remain in the grammar Schools or technical Schools and who later, with the help of public money, train for the professions. Therefore, visits to typical Nursery Schools – (for those under 5 years of age;) Infant and Junior Schools – (5–11 year olds;) Secondary Modern Schools (11–15 or 16;) Grammar or Technical Schools (11–18) and of course, Special Schools for handicapped children were arranged.

To help explain how attempts for this task of giving all children an equal opportunity in education and of helping them to reach the

Tea party for Colonial teachers at the Colonial Office.
A party of 33 teachers from Malaya, Sarawak, Singapore, Hong-Kong and North Borneo were entertained to tea by the Secretary of State for the Colonies (Mr. James Griffiths) on June 8th. 1951. They were accompanied by their Principal, Miss N. Dickinson.

fullest realisation of their personality, discussions were held in College for some of the ideas fundamental to human development, the importance of the individual child, the effect of the environment upon it, the need for encouragement to experiment and to develop initiative and the need for security. Miss Dickinson said we all need to acknowledge education to be so much more than class teaching for the purpose of installing knowledge.

Doubts about the wisdom of allowing each institution to draw up its own syllabus and programme might have surfaced, but the individuality of schools and colleges is traditional in England.

Miss Dickinson said, some of the visits might have given the students, a greater insight into our traditional democracy, our customs and our central and local government. We exchanged views on the part played by the ordinary citizens in the running of the country – elected Members of Parliament, the Mayor, Councillors and Local Government Officials, the Managers and Governors of the schools, the women's committees which foster women's interests and even the autonomous youth clubs.

It must all have seemed a fast moving and hazy kaleidoscope, but we, in a land which, in spite of vast tracts of open country, is heavily industrial, with huge cities (relieved, it is true, by green parks and flower gardens) have indeed a more complex problem. We felt that the more you saw for yourselves, the more you would understand and appreciate this problem and from the difficulties we have experienced find, perhaps, some helpful key to the future development of your own territories.

To understand us well you could not have left us without seeing something of our aesthetic heritage our theatres, concerts, galleries, Oxford, Cambridge, the Stratford Memorial Theatre, Covent Garden, the Albert Hall, the National Gallery and the Tate. And, of course, it was the Festival Year, so you saw something more of our cultural past and of contemporary effort.

We wish you could have stayed longer, for we had all too little time to learn of your own lands and to enjoy your friendship, but the sympathy and quick understanding which came from living together is, I feel sure, another example of the true education which comes from associating with other human beings, and for all who wish for a more peaceful world, we cannot deny the power of that sympathy and understanding.

I.N.DICKINSON.
Principal. 1951.

The visiting teachers/students on the front lawn of Wall Hall.

Visits Organised for the Students

An evening at a Women's Institute; Windsor Castle and Eton.

Visiting English villages – Denman College; Bottisham Village College; Papworth Village; and a Country Dance Party.

Festival of Britain Service at Aldenham Church.

South Bank Exhibition; Battersea Pleasure Gardens; and the Science Exhibition.

Meeting Queen Elizabeth (King George V1's wife) at St. Paul's Walden Bury.

Visiting English towns – Hitchin; meeting the Mayor at Watford; attending the Local Magistrates' Court, Watford;

Garston Youth Club.

Visiting factories – Blawnox (machinery of all types;) Granose Foods (health foods)

Empire Youth Rally at Watford.

A trip across London to Poplar to see the Festival of Britain Architecture Exhibition – passing Hendon, Kenton, Hampstead, the West End and East End.

The Houses of Parliament; The Imperial Institute; a Sight-seeing trip to London – visits to Westminster Abbey; the Tower of London; St. Paul's Cathedral; and Trafalgar Square; Kew Gardens; London Zoo; Hatfield House.

English Schools and Colleges – Infant Welfare Clinic; Watford Nursery School; Infant Schools – Malvern Way, Monkfrith and Stanburn; Junior Schools; Barclay Secondary Modern; Watford Grammar School for Girls; Special School – Gisbourne House Approved School for Girls; Chorleywood School for Blind Children; The Royal National Orthopaedic Hospital – (a crippled

Miss Margaret Davies (centre front) pictured with various students.

child gets his/her full share of education too.)
College visits – Homerton Training College; Balls Park; Wall Hall College Dance; Wall Hall Garden Party.
University Colleges – Cambridge, Kings College Chapel; Trinity College and St. John's College; Queen's College.
Oxford – Pembroke College; Merton College and Magdalen College. *Theatres* – Stratford, "Richard 11"; "Hamlet", The New Theatre; "Caesar and Cleopatra", St. James' Theatre; "Tosca", Covent Garden; Royal Philharmonic Orchestra conducted by Sir Thomas Beecham at The Albert Hall; The Lanchester Puppets, at Watford Grammar School; The Festival Ballet at the Stoll performing "The Nutcracker Suite" with the troupe led by Alicia Markova.

Reception by the Secretary of State for the Colonies – 8th. June Colonial Office, London.
The Students, Miss Dickinson and two other members of Wall Hall Staff, were invited to take tea with the Right Honourable Mr James Griffiths M.P., Secretary of State for the Colonies. They were introduced to him and members of the Colonial Office staff.

The Brains Trust – after the ten week course, it was decided that it would be of considerable value to discuss the information that had been gathered, this took the form of a Brains Trust. Chairman – Mr Newsom, Director of Education for Hertfordshire; Miss Gwilliam, Educational Advisor to the Colonial Office; Miss Dickinson, Principal of Wall Hall; Miss Pearce, Vice Principal of Wall Hall; Miss Goodison, History Lecturer, Wall Hall.

THE MALAYSIAN TEACHERS – 1951

A FAREWELL ADDRESS TO THE TEACHERS FROM OVERSEAS BY THE STAFF.

A year ago it would have seemed unbelievable that our hope of having South East Asian teachers at Wall Hall should ever be fulfilled. When the time came for us to bid you farewell it was a "sour-sweet" occasion, for the reality had far exceeded our expectations; you came to us as strangers but quickly became our friends; we found no barriers, but instead, common bonds which link one human being to another: family life, humour, ideals and in our case, a common profession and an interest in children. Whilst we showed to you, as honestly as we could, our English way of life, with all its achievements, failures and problems, we also learnt from you about peoples and a way of life of which we were comparatively ignorant. This proved a deep experience for us.

Queen Elizabeth (later the Queen Mother) with Miss Nancy Dickinson when the students visited St. Paul's Waldenbury in 1951

Although we are sad at losing you, we have so much of permanent value left: our many happy memories of your smiles and laughter, your colourful dresses, your hospitality and exciting food, your persistent shopping, the inevitable photographs and, what we value most, a widened understanding in the Eastern world.

It was as friends that we entertained you at our "Farewell At Home", together with those other people from Hertfordshire who had taken such pleasure and interest in your visit and had helped to make possible for you so many valuable experiences. When the Honourable Mrs. David Bowes-Lyon spoke to you on behalf of the Governors of the College, the Mayor for the Borough of Watford, Mr Baxter for the Local Education Authority, Mr Brothers for the teachers of Hertfordshire and Miss Dickinson for the College, you must have realised how much your stay had meant to us all and how much we hoped it had meant to you, not only personally, but in the contribution you will make to your own educational and social problems.

Queen Elizabeth meeting Malayan Students in 1951.

"Farewell England" – a response from A.S.Chong, North Borneo.

It is sad and strange that you have to say farewell to a place when you have just begun to feel at home in it. Such a lovely and comfortable place where the trees and flowers seem to beckon so winningly and where the whole atmosphere seems to wrap you so cosily. I cannot help the heartstrings being plucked and the lump rising in my throat when coming face to face with the fact – "Farewell England."

At the same time I am aware too that whatever tribute or compliment I may pay to her will all be superfluous and superficial – how can a sojourner of three months, such as I, do justice to a country resounding with the great names of Shakespeare, of Newton and Bernard Shaw? A country where the whole land seems to be a park and a sensible and good humoured family to boot!

However, here in my mind for England are: the massive, craggy buildings of Westminster Abbey and Cambridge, the River Avon, the village houses, snuggly settled beneath trees and last of all, the modern schools, where every child is given the opportunity to develop. These pictures I shall always treasure and at which the emotions of admiration will always fill one's heart at the sight of something beautiful and great.

CHAPTER 8

THE 10TH ANNIVERSARY 1955

TYPED COPY FROM THE TIMES EDUCATIONAL
SUPPLEMENT, 27 MAY 1955.

Ten years ago Wall Hall, a country house, set in beautiful gardens and parklands at Aldenham in Hertfordshire, was opened as the first Womens' Emergency College in the country. In the still uncertain days of war, the Staff and Students, under Miss K. M. Balfern, the first Principal, had many difficulties to contend with, but the College, administered by the Hertfordshire County Council, was successfully established and in 1949 it was made permanent. On 14 May it celebrated the 10th. anniversary of its official opening by Mr R. A. Butler, then Minister of Education. Past and present students, with guests from the Ministry of Education, the Hertfordshire Authority, the Cambridge Institute of Education and the schools, took part in the day's events. During the afternoon there was a ceremony in the college hall when the Chairman of the Governors, Mrs.F. H. Wales, on behalf of the County Council, presented a plaque to commemorate the establishment of the College. Mr J. F. Wolfenden, Vice Chancellor of Reading University, as the guest speaker, suggested that the day of celebration should be regarded as a time to look back with enjoyment on what had been accomplished and forward with fresh strength on what was to come. On this happy day, each teacher present should resolve to udertake three duties with fresh courage :- to keep an alive mind in spite of blunting routines; to enhance the reputation of the teaching profession; and, above all, to try to give children stability in an uncertain and bewildering world. The duty to the child raised certain suprememly difficult and delicate questions. The teacher had to decide what he should undertake and what should be left to the parent and whether he should share his beliefs and views with those he taught (*right*) 10th Anniversary Dinner Menu – 14th. May 1955.

WALL HALL
1945 — 1955

ALDENHAM PARISH CHURCH
SATURDAY, MAY 14th, 1955

WALL HALL TRAINING COLLEGE
1945 — 1955

Tenth Anniversary Dinner
14th May, 1955

MENU

SPRING VEGETABLE SOUP
CUTLETS IN ASPIC GARNISHED
SALAD
VANILLA CHARTREUSE
CHEESES
CIDER CUP   COFFEE

TOASTS
HER MAJESTY THE QUEEN

THE MINISTRY OF EDUCATION
THE SCHOOLS
THE GOVERNORS AND COUNTY COUNCIL
THE CAMBRIDGE INSTITUTE OF EDUCATION
THE COLLEGE

10th Anniversary Dinner at Wall Hall. From left to right (with backs to the fireplace) Miss Pearce (Vice Principal) John Newsom (Director of Education) Miss Margaret Davies (Art) J. Wolfendon (Vice Chancellor, Reading) Miss Nancy Dickinson (second Principal) A gentleman guest Miss Kathleen Balfern (first Principal)

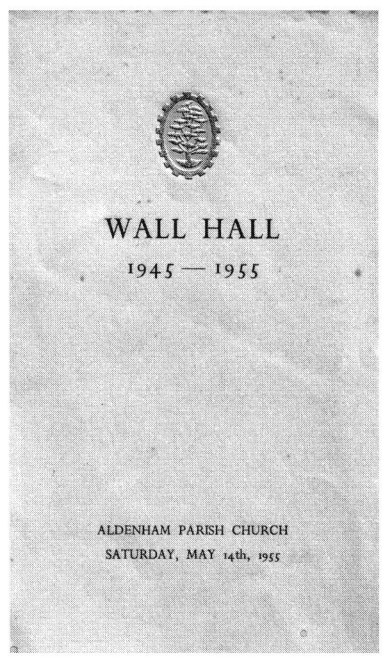

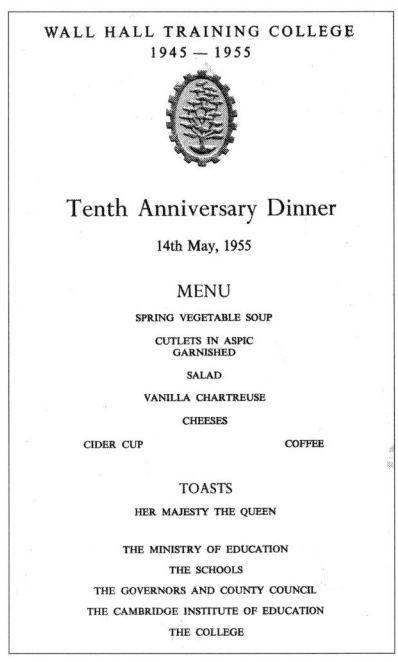

or hold back because of his pupil's immaturity. In Mr Wolfenden's opinion the desire to be dispassionate could lead to dishonesty, for it was dishonest to appear to have no beliefs. If the teacher was not honest, the children would not value honesty either. Mr Wolfenden emphasized that the refreshment of this anniversary should renew hopes and ideals so that they could be pursued again more wisely and with fresh life.

Typed copy from the Watford Observer – May 29th. 1955.

… because of the overcrowding in the Wall Hall Training College to hear the speech of Mr J. F. Wolfenden, an overflow meeting was held in a subsidiary hall, to which the Speaker's voice was relayed. Even the overflow assembly was a large one, many teachers sitting with their backs to the loudspeaker enjoying the humour and absorbing wisdom of Mr Wolfenden.

Earlier in the day, Mr W. O. Bell, Director of the Cambridge Institute of Education, gave the address at a service in Aldenham Church and later a plaque was presented to Miss I.N.Dickinson, the present Principal, by Mrs. F. H. Wales, Chairman of the Board of Governors.

WALL HALL 1945-1955
ORDER OF SERVICE - ALDENHAM PARISH CHURCH

Saturday, 14th. May 1955

Introduction
We are gathered here to offer to Almighty God our worship, our praise and our thanksgivings. To rejoice together at the completion of the first decade of our common life and to dedicate ourselves to His service and the education of His children in the years which lie ahead. Let us, therefore, lift up our hearts and sing.

Hymn   Praise to the Lord, the Almighty.
Reading   Ecclesiasticus 44, verses 1–14
         "Let us now praise famous men......"

A Litany of Work
Almighty God, Creator of the Universe and Maker of Man: we praise Thee that Thy Son, our Lord Jesus Christ, was a worker acquainted with daily toil; that it was He who said, My father worketh hitherto and I work; and, again, I must work the works of Him that sent me; and, again, I have finished the work which Thou gavest me to do:
For our belief that it was the purpose of God which called us into being, that we too might work the works of Him that sent us:
        We thank Thee Lord.
For the privilege of being called to share in Thy purpose for the world in our generation and for the desire in our hearts to respond to thy challenge:
        We thank Thee Lord.
For the opportunities of work which are ours even today and which, faithfully used, will fit us for a worthy life of service:
        We thank Thee Lord.
For the hopes Thou hast implanted within us of becoming useful members of society and citizens worthy to exert an influence upon our times:
        We thank Thee Lord.
For the dignity of honest toil, the joy of achievement and the honour of attaining an acknowledged goal:
        We thank Thee Lord.
For the opportunity to contribute, by our work now and in the future, to the happiness and well-being of those we love and especially of all the children in our care:

We thank Thee Lord.
For the knowledge that He who worked with His hands and brain, who knew the weariness of physical toil and the high exaltation of sustained thinking, was tempted in all points as we are, yet did not fail:
We praise thee O God and bless Thy name.

Collect
Eternal God, the light of the minds that know Thee, the joy of the hearts that love Thee and the strength of the wills that serve Thee: grant us so to know Thee that we may truly love Thee, so to love Thee that we may fully serve Thee, whose service is perfect freedom.
The Lord's Prayer   (to be sung)

Anthem	Jesu, joy of man's desiring. J.S.Bach.
Reading	1 Romans 12. Translation by J.B.Phillips. Verses 1–9
Hymn	Immortal, invisible, God only wise.
Address	W. O. Bell, M.A.
	Director of the Cambridge Institute of Education.
	Text – What doth the Lord require of thee. Micah.
Hymn	Fill Thou my life, O Lord my God.
Blessing	
Epilogue	(to be sung kneeling)
	God be in my head, and in my understanding.
	God be in mine eyes, and in my looking.
	God be in my mouth, and in my speaking.
	God be at mine end, and at my departing.
	Anonymous. Sarum Missal.

WALL HALL 1945-1955

Summary of Courses and Number of Studentsand Administration and Examinations.

May 1945 to June 1946 – First Emergency Training   88
Scheme Course.
Administered by the Herts. County Council for the Ministry of Education. Examined by the Ministry of Education.

Aug.1946 to Sept. 1947 – Second Emergency Training   125
Scheme Course.
Administered by the Herts. County Council for the Ministry of Education . Examined by the Ministry of Education.

Oct.1947 to Nov. 1948 – Third Emergency Training   122
Scheme Course.

Administered by the Herts. County Council for the Ministry of Education. Examined by the Ministry of Education.

Jan. 1949 to Feb. 1950 – Fourth Emergency Training 48
Administered by the Herts. County Council for the Ministry of Education. Examined by the Ministry of Education.

Jan. 1949 to July 1950 – First Two Year Course 48
(5 terms)
Established as a permanent College administered by the Herts. County Council from January 1949. Examined by the CambridgeLocal Examinations Syndicate and the Ministry of Education.

April 1950 to March 1951 – First Two Year Course 32
for experienced teachers. Examined by the Ministry of Education.

April 1950 to July 1952 – Second Two Year Course 56
Examined by the Cambridge Institute of Education.

April 1951 to July 1951 – Special Course for Teachers from 25 the Far East. Sponsored by the Colonial Office, The Ministry of Education and Herts. County Council.

Sept. 1951 to July 1953 – Third Two Year Course 46 Examined by the Cambridge Institute of Education.

Sept. 1952 to July 1954 – Fourth Two Year Course 60 Examined by the Cambridge Institute of Education.

Sept. 1953 to July 1954 – Present Students 50
Examined by the Cambridge Institute of Education.

Sept. 1954 to July 1954 – Present Students 58
Examined by the Cambridge Institute of Education.

WALL HALL 1945–1955.
ADDITIONS OR CHANGES TO THE BUILDINGS.

May 1945 to June 1946 – Main buildings, Otterspool and Laboratory in use.

September 1946 – Red House added.

July 1947 – P.E. Hall completed.

J. F. Wolfenden, Vice Chancellor of Reading University with Miss Nancy Dickinson, Principal of Wall Hall College and John Newsom, County Education Officer for Hertfordshire.
14 May 1955

An aerial view in 1951 of Wall Hall Mansion and Estate Gardens. Note the various vegetable gardens and greenhouses.

14 May 1955.
Miss Nancy Dickinson [right] receiving a plaque of the opening of Wall Hall College, when Wall Hall became a permanent College and was no longer an Emergency College. On behalf of the County, the plaque was presented by the Chairman of Governors.

1947–1949 – Minor alterations; additional windows; room partitions.

1949–1950 – Greenhouses converted to temporary Craft rooms. Partial lighting of drives.

September 1950 – Holbrook added.

October 1950 – New kitchen; pantry and larder built.

November 1950 – Alterations to Dining Hall. Central heating installed.

December 1950 – College bus.

January 1951 – New cloakroom opened.
Conversion of Library. Exchange of Ministry of Supply furniture for divan beds; stackable chairs; fireside chairs.

July 1951 – Conversion of greenhouses to bicycle sheds.

April 1952 – Stable block opened.

May 1952 – Open air theatre completed.

November 1952 – P.E. Hall improved; floor, windows, redecoration.

1954 – New hockey field prepared. Additional lighting of drives.

1955 – New hard tennis court to be laid.

CHAPTER 9

MEMORIES OF WALL HALL

MEMORIES OF WALL HALL
FROM THE WALL HALL ASSOCIATION NEWSLETTER
1995-96

Kay Davies – Principal (1966-81)
I first saw Wall Hall in 1965 when I drove up to the Mansion door for interview. Though I knew of the College, I had no idea of the attraction of the site. There it was; an impressive pseudo-gothic house with its interesting past, most recently the American Association – and still in evidence, furniture once belonging to the Pierpont Morgans. Fine surroundings with at least a remnant of Parkland. The early fall of an old tree encouraged me to plant a replacement, a tulip tree and this encouraged a number of subsequent similar gestures – now sadly difficult to identify after the theft of the inscriptions! Surely all who worked at Wall Hall then, retain fond memories of a gracious environment in a quiet rural setting. I recall, as no doubt others will, seeing foxes, muntjac deer and the sight from my office window of a great variety of birds. There was an annual profusion of daffodils and narcissi to be enjoyed, plus the May meadow carpeted with cowslips and in the Spinney the haze of bluebells and the splendid azaleas.

New building was in evidence, the Binghams and a Central Block was complete. The Education Building was next on the agenda. I was told on my first visit of an intended increase in numbers to about 700 students, very soon after amended to 1,000, though that was not attained until after the merger with Balls Park. Practically all my time at the College was taken up with the pressure of increasing numbers and building plans. Academic changes came fast too, the Certificate Course to the BEd, via a brief encounter

"Rag Day" 1970, Watford. Dillon the goat (reared by Cheryll Hall) in white.

with London University then Cambridge University and ultimately the more autonomous CNAA.

On that first visit I met Miss Dickinson, who was a hard act to follow and Miss Roberts and Miss Bagley, responsible for high standards of Housekeeping and Catering. There were no students to be seen as it was still vacation. Before long men students were to be recruited and they brought a new liveliness and some problems. Changing social patterns gave students a more liberal quality of residential life and evidence of greater maturity for the most part. Older students were always a feature of Wall Hall and did much to give it a particular character and accounted for the strong and continuing 'Old Students' Association'. Through its newsletter and Annual Meeting many friendships have been maintained and this is true too of the flourishing Field Group with its extended membership.

Throughout my time, overall responsibility for the College rested with the Hertfordshire County Council, an enlightened body compared with many others. Even so, there was never much money around and yet colleagues, thanks to good management by Bursars and others, kept standards going. It was sometimes difficult for staff and Students with reasonable requests for more resources or better facilities, to have to be denied them.

In spite of all the problems, the threats, some realities, of mergers, closures, contractors – we maintained a reputation for quality and innovation and were wholeheartedly supported by the schools of the area with whom we worked closely. We were early into closed circuit television, foreign student exchanges, we opened up a nursery school and developed some of the first courses in the special needs and education of the deaf fields. The great expansion of in-service training in the 70's brought in many teachers for evening courses, leading to Advanced Degrees for a good number. The first move towards non-teaching degrees came at the end of my time and led to a close association with Hatfield Polytechnic. Wall Hall was for me a very happy experience, though far more hectic and pressurised and problem beset, than I have ever anticipated on that first visit. Such is the way of higher Education! Colleagues and Students were an able and richly varied community, it was a privilege to be with them and I value the links which continue.

Richard Wheeler
My first impression of Wall Hall takes me back to the Spring of 1965 when I came for interview for a post in the History Department. I remember getting lost and taking the Otterspool Drive turning which, of course, gave me an excellent view of the Mansion. I was interviewed by Nancy Dickinson, who later telephoned me and said "You're very young Mr Wheeler, but we will take a gamble on you." I thought Wall Hall looked good for two or three years but I ended up staying for 27 years, so I hope that the gamble paid off! I remember the Staff Room and Mansion and the new buildings which had just been completed. The first term ended with Nancy Dickinson's retirement and a Staff party, including a photograph which still brings back happy memories.

Over the years I enjoyed the History Department – my colleagues – Joan Hill, Trevor May, Sheila Fletcher, Mike Williams, Julia Bush, Tony McCulloch and later, colleagues from Balls Park – Alan Lawrence, Paul Gatland, Alan Thomson, and others and of course successive generations of students, both youngsters and matures. They were happy and fruitful years.

I remember the building of the swimming pool and all the years that my children and their friends enjoyed the pool and the grounds during the hot summers (and some rainy ones) in the seventies and eighties. The merger of Balls Park and Wall Hall was a climactic event in the 70's; the CNAA, collaboration with Polytechnic, the development of the BA Combined Studies Degree and finally the merger with the Polytechnic in 1987, ending with incorporation into the University of Hertfordshire in 1992, together constitute a chapter in educational history.

I was fortunate to work closely with some agreeable and stimulating colleagues – under Kay Davies' leadership from 1966 onwards, as deputy to Derek Haslam from 1981 and latterly under Neil Buxton's leadership from 1988 – until I finally jumped off the end of the pier in 1992 after four and a half years as Dean of the School of Humanities and Education with responsibility for the Wall Hall campus.

My colleagues and students – too numerous to mention by name – made working at Wall Hall a labour of love over the years. I

"Rosie" the pig – November 1981.

Young children feeding one of the goats. Rural Studies photographs sent by Mary Hood.

always counted myself fortunate to work in such pleasant surroundings and in such congenial company. The continuation of teacher Education on the Wall Hall campus – at one time against expectations – and the expansion of opportunities signified by the development of Humanities and in-service provision, remains an achievement with which I am proud to be associated.

Joan Stampe
My 16 happy years at Wall Hall (1955–71) have now been well exceeded by equally happy years of retirement, but the memories of those years remain with me vividly; the welcome of Miss Dickinson and the Staff; the Staff Room with its silk clad walls, where we used to congregate – all eleven of us (academic) plus administrative staff; the red plush top of the fireguard where most of us could perch and warm our backsides (was there a fire, or is that a bit of embroidery?) the old lab. in Holbrook; the view of the river and beyond (no M1 then) from my room in Otterspool; the few calm years before the great expansion began; its bit by bit planning. (I recall the year we produced plans for expansion to 250 students and another set for 400 students – we got 300!)

Finally the Holbrook Lab. was given over to Health Education, the small livestock spilled over into what had been Miss Fairweather's sitting-room, with connecting door to the new Science/Geography block, with a ground floor suite of Labs. tutorial rooms, preparation rooms, etc., plus the Rural Science area behind the Farmhouse and the Staff of the Science Department nearly equalled the size of the whole academic staff when I arrived in 1955.

The expansion provided lots of interest (and many frustrations) over continuous planning; new buildings and equipment, new Staff appointments – sometimes in halves – and always more students to interview; all these preparations for an increasing intake carried on while catering for the current population, with its approved Staff/Student ratio.

But there were excitements and fun too; the advent of the pig (and later the calf) the lamb who spent a summer vacation in Kent and made an historic transfer from father's car to my Austin 'Countryman' beside Admiralty Arch (hardly a lamb any more!) The goats which defied all regulations at Waterloo and Liverpool Station – some will recall trying to keep lively kids on the balance long enough to be weighed, the one who knocked over a whole pile of biscuit tins – no one counted the biscuits which quickly disappeared – one who consumed several evening papers neatly stacked in the luggage van (well not so stacked after her annoyance had been vented on them.) One could go on about the travel adventures of the goats, which ceased of course once Mary Hood was established in the Rural Science department. But I must mention all the children who came to see and handle the animals and to fish in the pond – children who had never touched a guinea pig, and some who thought all milk came out of bottles.

How sad, that just when the nation has become Environmental conscious, the Rural Science and Biogeography courses have been deemed expendable – but perhaps the teachers (and parents) who shared our interest in countryside matters are still nurturing seeds of interest amongst the young. It is heartening that the Old Students' Field Group is flourishing and still waving the Environmental flag.

Joan Hill
My first memory of Wall Hall is walking up the drive for my interview. The butcher stopped and gave me a lift. As he put me down, he said "you'll do" even though he did not know what for. I arrived in 1960 to a small community, compared with school, and situated in lovely surroundings. Everyone was friendly and helpful. I think it took a year to begin to understand the real workings of the place despite the perpetual exchange of ideas among staff. This was something we tried to preserve as college expanded. Garden parties, college engagements and formal dinner for staff and students are all part of the early memories.

Expansion came soon after 1961, it seemed that change/adaption of courses either in one's specialism or in the general courses was a constant characteristic. Then, after 1970, with the threatened contraction of colleges, we started to plan the best deployment of staff talents. The introduction of the B.Ed. meant links with the London Institute and even stronger links with Cambridge. Memories are many but some incidents emerge: the student from a town who had not seen a milk churn; the student on a field day who thought parts of Coventry Cathedral looked like pegs in a school cloakroom; the mature student who said sadly that I had made her ask 'why?' so much that she could not just relax and enjoy something; a member of staff who on hearing this agreed with the comment, that if she had said that she used S.R. toothpaste, I would have asked why!(Exaggeration!) the field trip when someone was driven home ill and shaded by an umbrella; the students who stood guard to catch a Peeping Tom when the " Wall Hall detectives" sat in a car on the drive, determined to end the nuisance and success was the reward; the students who obviously timed my progress to bed so that one night when I was off-duty they declared there was a burglar in my flat, for I had put my light out too quickly; the impact of President Kennedy's assassination upon students; the night the water tank at Otterspool burst and the ever faithful Mr Hart roared in to rescue us; fire drills and false alarms; shared fun in the swimming pool; students battling with dissertations and the reward at the interview; students' generous hard work in putting up exhibitions; school practice – its heartaches and success; the mini – skirt era when one Head was convinced that the student was respectable because the student wore tights; lodgings; the advent of men students and the first mixed hostel.

Occasions marked by Mr Worthy and his camera; he was nothing to Mr Thompson and Mr May when they made a video for the 1970's Open days – it was fun to be a Victorian for a while. One can only mention a few memories of staff; Miss M. E. Davies with her 'straight eye'; Miss Pearce with her astringent wit; Mr Wheeler returning with the Stuarts; Miss Roberts and the flowers; Mrs. Paske and her white medicines; Miss Bagley with her confections; Miss Boyle and the pancakes; Mrs. Haigh's teasing about my use of eyebrows to bring in the sleepy back row; Mrs. Hill and the gym floor; fabulous parties and endless extravagant fun; Miss Dickinson with her care and thought in the building extensions and Miss Davies with her disciplined influence over courses and planning and both with their personal interest in everyone. These are only some memories that flood in, but as I reflect it is the fun, friendship, hard work of all which colour my thoughts. I remember the happy farewell and the joy of everyone at my marriage in 1971.

Kay Roberts, Domestic Bursar
From 1962–1981, almost half the life of the College and what changes we lived through. During the recent winter when the snow was piled high everywhere I looked, I recalled the day in January 1962 when I arrived at Wall Hall. The then narrow causeway was waist high with snow, only passable with difficulty and the drive to the courtyard even worse. In those days some domestic work was done by resident Finnish girls, they had decorated in their traditional way with glowing candles in tiny igloos, which made a very cheery welcome. The following winter we were again snowed up just as term began. Miss Dickinson led all the resident students and staff outside to clear the snow and we had a lot of fun. Would it happen today?

Memories of Wall Hall

My abiding memory of my first day at college, was of the college bus; it was so incredibly uncomfortable with its rigid wooden-slatted seats, that the journey from Bushey and Oxhey seemed to take forever. The thought of the beautiful mansion, where Miss Pearce had interviewed me, was still quite fresh in my mind and I nervously wondered what my room-mate would be like and where our room would be situated.

I consider myself very fortunate to have been in South with Miss Margaret Davies as hostel warden. She was such a kind, approachable and understanding lady who, like me, had a love of dogs. Ben the corgi was getting elderly by this time and hated to be left alone, so he accompanied us to Art classes and always managed to sit by those who had a liking for him! I sometimes "baby sat" him for the odd weekend and, despite his somewhat unpredictable temper, he was always very good – even when he had to be carried up and down the stairs. Miss Davies managed to bring out even the tiniest artistic streak in us all. Sometimes I wondered how she could look at our work and see some hope there. When she could think of nothing special to say, she would gently nod her head and say "Oh, how interesting!"

From left to right :- Dilys Morgan; Gillian Martin-Dye; Rosalind Roberts; Enid Weston and Carole-Ann Wells.

Students who were in Red House 1952–1954. Photo by Wendy Grune, 115 Preston New Road, Southport. PR9 8PA. *Back Row* – Pamela Symons; ? Margaret Pearce; Margery Dower; Ruth May; Wendy Grune; ? Mary Tutt. *Centre Row* – Eileen O'Sullivan; Mary Marriot; Miss Firth; Miss Bailey; Dorothy Webster; Mary Emett. *Front Row* – ? ?

For a few years after I had left college, Miss Davies had a summer course for old students and we painted to our heart's delight in the beautiful gardens; needless to say, trees featured heavily in all our works of art! Shapes and shadows came to life, so many shades of green, small details and inconsistencies all contributed to new experiences.

In the old greenhouse, I was introduced to needlecraft and Pottery; my coil pot lasted many years of flower arranging before it finally got broken when I moved house. Miss Fairweather, ever serious, would say of someone who had done some needlecraft particularly well, "Have you done it before?" She also explained to us why we were not allowed men in our rooms after 8 p.m. – because their passions were stronger and our resistance was lower after that time!

Although I was not talented at singing, I joined the choir in order to get my room-mate and others to join in something else (which now eludes me). I found sight-reading difficult, but Miss Croall was a good teacher and music was a relief from so much written work. There were also performances to enjoy, the highlight being the production of Dido and Aeneas which was staged in the dell. The dell was also the place where Miss Dickinson would coach us in using our voices efficiently. It was a peaceful place where students could escape to read or reflect.

In my second year Miss Thompson (now Mrs. Hill) returned from a sabbatical year to put a spark into our P.E. and Dance. She inspired us – well, some of us – to take part in Open day performances and I recall leaping around to Danse Macabre on the side lawn on a beautiful summer's day. I'm not sure if I danced what I was supposed to as being without my glasses meant groping in the fog, but we were well applauded. Education lectures were made enjoyable by Mr Worthy who was fresh from teaching in schools and knew a trick or two for getting the attention of the class of unruly children. His practical approach stood us in good stead for teaching practice; but I have to admit to nearly throwing it all in when, after my first lesson of my first practice, the class teacher presented me with a long list of all my mistakes! I vowed that I would never do this to a student and I kept that promise throughout my thirty two years of teaching.

Of course my favourite time was in the Biology laboratory. My first sight of Joan Stampe was in there and she was happily cleaning out Timothy, the hamster's cage! Lectures took place in the Holbrook laboratory and were always very practically orientated; we were encouraged by Joan's enthusiasm. She had as amazing ability to recognise bird – song even whilst driving her car! Her love of all things in the natural world left us all with an enduring respect for the environment.

Miss Bailey with another group of Students.

We were well cared for during our sojourn at college. We had to be in our hostels at 10 p.m. but we could sign out until midnight providing a friend in the hostel would be a referee. This meant reporting your absence, if you had not returned by that time, in case something had happened to you. The food cooked in the dining room was excellent as we often had fresh vegetables and fruit from the greenhouses and walled garden. On Fridays we collected our weekend rations from the pantry and were left to our own devices as to how we prepared them – not that too much could be achieved with a tin of corned beef hash and endless eggs. Matron saw to our health needs, wielding a rather thick needle with which to dispense antibiotics and the like. She did not encourage malingerers, but if you were really unwell her fierceness melted. Matron had a cat who had only a stump for a tail and he was relentlessly bombarded by birds who seemed to tease him. He was black and white and so often slept on the coal that his appearance was grey. As he lived in the mansion somewhere, we in South saw him often and he became quite friendly.

The two years were not only filled with work; we had college dances and *men* were invited, especially from Newlands Park Teacher Training College for men. Most of them just lounged around and, as in those days women did not dance together, there was not much chance of getting a dance; rather a poor show when you consider how much time we had spent getting into our party best and stiletto heels! We also made sorties into Watford which was a day's outing by bus, but it had the lure of the picture house, coffee houses and pleasant window shopping. During the summer in the beautiful Italian garden we were allowed to sunbathe (discreetly) read, practise drama, gossip with friends or visitors or just sleep. It was an oasis of calm offering reflection on times past when Wall Hall was a private dwelling. The photograph shows some of my friends in 1960 in the Italian garden.

Before we left Wall Hall to face the classroom alone, we were all taken by coach to Cambridge – the university to which we were affiliated – for a special service of commemoration. It was awe-inspiring, wonderful and served to remind us how important and responsible our new roles would be.

Pat Saunders (*nee* Insall) 1959–1961.

Memories of Wall Hall 1955–57 *-reflections* 2002.

The overwhelming memory is of the sheer charm and ambience of Wall Hall with its grand house, long drive and splendid gardens. I feel now as I did then, that we were privileged to live in such a lovely setting to observe the changing seasons.

My first home was in the major bedroom above the entrance hall shared with Lynne, Barbara and Pauline (surnames escape me.) After a few weeks we were moved into the bedroom on the far left which was deemed to be larger. It had a tower with a doorway in a corner, rumoured to have been used by students returning after lock-up time as the only available entrance to the building. On a cold, snowy January night I celebrated my 21st. birthday in this room. My next move was to a recently vacated single room in East Wing where we could hear the stable clock chime during the night. We used the main staircase to the ground floor and all meals were taken in the beautiful wood panelled dining room. There lecturers joined us for lunch, the students deferentially stood awaiting their arrival and, one lecturer to each table said grace before the meal, it was intended to promote intelligent conversation and allow the staff to get to know the students. Supper was a more casual meal, though senior students often had notices of future events and general information to read out. I have vivid memories of end of term balls in this magnificent hall; the library was on the left, with memories of time researching reference books and writing essays. Opposite was the Common Room and beyond there was the Music Room where occasional music evenings were held – a special memory is of Anthony Hopkin, pianist and composer, singing and playing. Other interesting lecturers visited: Brian Vesey-Fitzgerald opened our minds to the life of spiders and actor John Laurie, later famed as Private Frazer of Dad's Army, gave a lively poetry reading in the P.E. Hall. Coffee and tea-breaks were taken in the main entrance hall or Common Room. At the front of the house on the first floor of the main building was the Sick Bay, with Matron in attendance and the rooms of the Principal, Miss Dickinson were on the right hand side above the Music Room; I believe Miss Pearce, the Vice Principal, also lived in main building. The other lecturers were hostel wardens each allocated to a hostel, in my time these were: Main House; East Wing; Stable Block; Otterspool (a lovely house for art study,) Farm House and Red House in Aldenham village. There may have been more accommodation above the laboratories used for Environmental Studies located on the left between Main House and Farm seen upon leaving College.

Throughout my second year I lived at the red-brick Farm House. Bicycles were then a necessity as the drive to the main road was long; cycles were left at the caretaker's cottage by the main gates. A bus from the stop outside Aldenham Church took us into Bushey for a train to London for concert and theatre visits. I saw Richard Burton and John Neville in Othello at the Old Vic – they alternated roles of the Moor and Iago and I saw both, also Donald Houston as the narrator in Under Milk Wood, Carmen at The Royal Opera House, Covent Garden and our music lecturer singing in the Bach Choir at the Albert Hall at Christmas. We cycled to Otterspool for art lectures – in my first year my bike was kept in the old glasshouses at the side of the house on the left beside East Wing's back entrance to the Main building, the Main Entrance being reserved for more dignified visitors. The College bus was driven by the caretaker to take us to teaching Practice and Environmental visits.

In front of College a sports field was used for hockey and at the rear were tennis and netball courts and space for athletics, these were the domain of the Scots P.E. lecturer, Miss Thompson (I think) who also used the P.E. Hall at the rear of Main

Building to hone our P.E. teaching skills. Nearby, a large area of

"The Hunt" as it gathered on the lawn in front of the Mansion. Lord Aldenham's hounds *c* 1900

converted glasshouses were workshops for Pottery with kilns, needlework and other handcrafts.

Beyond, were the gardens with wonderful cedar trees and in the Spring, azaleas and rhododendrons in flower, the rose gardens, the pool and the 'Folly'. To the left the garden's Open Air theatre, known as The Dell for its dipping bowl shape where in my first Summer we performed The Antigone, which we dubbed The Agony for the mosquito bites suffered while waiting off stage behind bushes, despite being armed with a Flit gun!

For relaxation we walked through the woods and fields outside the Park and gardens. College always seemed to throb with life, there was so much to do, so many deadlines to meet, but always lots of fun in good company. The social highlights were the mid and end of term dances and we enjoyed other social events in the P.E. Hall. In my time it was an all female College which we jokingly referred to as the Virgin's Retreat – these were respectable times!

Mildred Sullivan 1955–57.

Memories of Wall Hall By Ruth Barden.

As a small child I used to visit Wall Hall with my father who was a florist in Watford. Mr Steward the head gardener at Wall Hall used to supply my father with flowers, but I remember the walled garden and the delicious nectarines! Another memory that has remained with me, is the pungent smell of the geranium plants in one of the potting sheds.

Little did I realise that I would one day return as a Mature Student. Sadly, my father died on September 1st. 1968, just a few weeks before I started my studies.

In my previous career as Housecraft advisor for the electrical industry, I was involved with schools in the district, giving demonstrations, talks and instructions for the Duke of Edinburgh's Award Scheme on the use and care of Electricity. A chance remark made to me by a young pupil during one of these courses was "It has been so interesting. Do you teach?" This comment sowed the seed for the decision to apply to Wall Hall at a later date, after I had been seriously ill and wished to make a fresh start.

Unable to have a family, I could not have chosen anything better. I looked at everything in life through the wonder of a child's eyes.

I enjoyed the atmosphere of the library in the Mansion and was thrilled one day to see a weasel just the other side of the window. Wall Hall also gave me the opportunity for my one and only stage appearance. I was on the Swimming Pool Fund Committee and an Old Time Music Hall was one of the fund-raising efforts. I was so nervous and terrified that I might forget the words of my song – "Why am I always the Bridesmaid?" I had the verse written on a card in my bouquet. Regarding other musical talents, I regret to write Recorder playing was certainly not evident in my case. Doreen Wager, a member of my group, usually shared a practice room with me and it was only necessary for one of us to pipe a wrong note and we were convulsed in a fit of giggles! Poor Mrs. Bell! I also had the misfortune to display an ink bottle on one of the Needlework tables during a lecture and for this demeanour I was severely reprimanded!

Happy days re. being a member of the Field Group. I only led one outing on 'The History of Lavenham, Suffolk' but I felt privileged to have had this opportunity.

Ruth Barden – Mature Student – 1968/70.

1961–64 Students Xmas dance

Winter 1964 Otterspool Libby Gillespie Smith on the frozen River Colne

Memories of Wall Hall From an ex-student.

I remember Miss M.Davies telling us that she crawled into a petrol station on a wing and a prayer, to find that she had 9 old pence in her pocket and this bought her a cup of petrol to get her car to College.

I remember Miss Fairweather and her enthusiasm for mummifying her needlework students in strips of sticky paper to make cheap instant tailor's dummies. Once the poor girls had petrified and the gummed paper had hardened, she set them free by cutting up the back of the tape and easing them out. Unfortunately, each time she did it, she cut up the girls' bras and pants in the process and when the girls complained, she breezily declared that it was of small consequence as they could easily buy some more. As poor students they were not happy about it. When Miss Fairweather had massacred all the students' undies she decided that she would like them to mummify her and produce a tailor's dummy for her. The girls only too readily agreed and carefully cut her out of not only the paper dummy, but her very costly foundation garment. Needless to say Miss Fairweather was horrified and rounded on the girls with vigour – to which they solemnly replied that it didn't matter as she could easily buy herself another corset! They felt a lot better after that.

Then there were the rural studies' students who had to milk the goats and never did learn how to stop the wretched goats kicking the bucket over as soon as they had finished being milked.

A student who was one of the last of the two year training writes: I shall always remember the wonderful Art lectures given by the late Margaret Davies. She always found something 'fascinating' in everyone's work. Now that I have time to do so, I have been attending classes in drawing and water-colour painting. She lives in my memory with great fondness together with her little corgi Ben, who often accompanied her to lectures.

I remember the performance of 'Dido and Aeneas' in the Dell. it was very hot at the first performance. I had to stand perfectly still holding a boar's head made of papier mache whilst my knee was being eaten by an insect. The second night a storm broke and the boar's head slowly sank as the water was absorbed. It was a wonderful experience – Miss Croall always got the best out of us: I remember the College Bus with its wooden slats for seats: Mr Worthy my

Education lecturer who gave so many practical tips which helped on teaching practice in a tough Secondary School. Finally, but not least, the daffodils!

Fond memories abound from Otterspool – Mr and Mrs. Ron Seward who were so kind to all the students – providing accommodation for visiting boyfriends – helping mend broken cars, etc.

A couple of incidents spring to mind, the first when we were on the top floor. My room mate was having difficulty opening the sash-cord window. Eventually it opened, but not before her arm went through the pane of glass and she ended up with a nasty cut which needed stitches. Our resident lecturer appeared with an item of 'feminine hygiene' minus the loops to wrap around the wound!

Summer 1963 Otterspool

Another year we were at the other end of the first floor with a balcony outside our room – we had a fire drill at 8 a.m. This was a frosty morning, in my haste to get out I broke a pane of glass. We must have looked a funny sight in our night attire huddled on the lawn. The fireman came one evening to give a demonstration and I was chosen to be carried down the ladder – he told me I was too tense!

Remember the bad winter of 1963. The river at Otterspool was frozen solid – we could slide and skate on there. The roads up to the College were frozen over – the trees were so beautiful – this went on for ten weeks and we were on teaching practice!

A colourful sight was Lord Aldenham's hunt in their 'pink' coats galloping across the grounds. Sometimes they were dressed in green for 'hare' coursing. Leslie Webb (a tutor) frequently went round unblocking the fox holes.

I enjoyed all the nature around and was fascinated to learn in a Geography lecture that a small pond in the woods at Otterspool marked the southerly edge of the Ice Age in England.

Perhaps the most amazing sight was to see a kingfisher at Otterspool – the colours were magnificent! (No signature)

CHAPTER 10

COLLEGE EXPANSION IN THE 1960s

Clearing the grounds for development – Central Block

COLLEGE EXPANSION IN THE 1960S

Central Block - Philosophy lecture rooms.

The drive leading to the Mansion with Refectory on the left.

The Gymnasium and Dance Studio

The Education Block - showing the Buttery in the bottom right hand corner, and the Nursery on the left of the photograph.

The Science Laborotories and Geography Department.

Binghams Student Accomodation.

The old Dairy Parlour

and Farmyard.

The former Dairy Parlour being used as Studios.

CHAPTER 11

COLLEGE FOUNDATION DAY CELEBRATIONS

WALL HALL COLLEGE FOUNDATION DAY 3 JUNE 1965.

The 20th. Anniversary of Wall Hall College, Aldenham and the completion of the present building phase, were celebrated on Thursday, 3 June 1965. The principle guests were Sir John Newsom C.B.E. and Miss Freda Gwilliam, Educational Advisor to the Ministry of Overseas Development, who was to deliver the Foundation Lecture in the new Central Hall. This accomodated large numbers of other guests, including representatives of the teaching profession, the administration, civic and other local organisations; past and present members of staff, representatives of past student years and the present students of the College.

The guests were welcomed by Alderman L. E. Haines, Chairman of the Governors and by Miss I. N. Dickinson B.A., the Principal for the past 18 years. Miss Dickinson thanked the many people concerned with the growth and development of the College, paying special tribute to Mr R. L. Pye of the Architect's Department of the Hertfordshire County Council for his work on the present phase of the building. She then introduced Sir John Newsom, who, as County Education Officer of the time, was responsible for the opening of the College.

In a short address, Sir John outlined how the Hertfordshire County Council came to acquire the Wall Hall estate on the death, in 1942, of its former owner, the American financier, Mr J. Pierpont Morgan. The Emergency Teacher Training Scheme suggested an obvious use for the building. It was thus that, in May 1945, Wall Hall became the first Emergency Training College for Women, with 90 students aged between 21 ans 41 under the first Principal, Miss K. M. Balfern.

20th Anniversary – Foundation Day Lecture. Students listening to Miss Freda Gwilliam's presentation.

Miss Freda Gwilliam, in the Foundation Lecture, took as her theme, the dual role of women in modern society – that of the home maker and that of the worker, contributing on equal terms with men. This dual role, though natural in many rural communities, had still to be fully accepted, although modern society could no longer afford to sacrifice the woman's contribution. Public opinion must be educated, first to accept the principle of the dual role and then to make adequate provision so that women can work harmoniously, and on equal terms, with men and still fulfil successfully their responsibilities in the home. For teachers there need be no conflict for, with proper consideration and planning to avoid difficulties, the married woman teacher can contribute most effectively to the needs of young people.

After a vote of thanks, proposed by the President of the Students' Union, Miss J. McRoberts, tea was taken in the new Dining Hall. This was followed by informal tours of the extensive new buildings. These will cater for 440 students in September, but the addition of a new Education Centre will allow the number of students to be increased to 600 by 1967.

WALL HALL COLLEGE, FOUNDATION LECTURE
3 JUNE 1965.

Alderman L. E. Haines, Chairman of the Governors, welcomed the guests and congratulated the College on its 20th. Anniversary.

Miss I. N. Dickinson, Principal, thanked individuals for the help they have given and introduced Sir John Newsom.

Sir John Newsom then introduced his talk by saying he had 9

minutes dead, so he would be unable to give much wisdom. He told how the College really began, the story that was never in the history books. Before the last war the County Council took an option of the whole estate for £200,000 and had to put down £14,000. Mr Pierpont Morgan died in 1942 and the problem was whether or not to take up the option. This resulted in the best debate that Sir John has ever heard at a County Council meeting. 1942 was a very black period of the war and the argument was that if we lose the war the present actions will not matter, if we win we shall have this large and valuable estate to put to the most suitable purpose. The figure quoted was, of course, a very considerable sum of money. Having made their decision, the Clerk of the County Council called in Sir John and said, "For God's sake think of some educational purpose we could use that blasted building for. If we can get past the Board of Education we might get some of the money back." On inspecting the building, it was found to be occupied by a highly secret branch of the Army, but the resulting conference suggested that it should be used for adult education. Wall Hall, with 37 acres, cost £15,000. The Emergency Training Scheme for teachers was put forward in 1943; in May 1944, it was suggested that Wall Hall should be used for that purpose and, after only 12 months, the College was opened with 90 students, aged between 21 and 41. Of these, 75% had been to Grammar Schools, but only 38% had a school certificate. Only the Principal, Miss K. M. Balfern, had any previous Training College experience – perhaps the success of the College was largely due to that fact. The Emergency Scheme continued for 4 years and then the College went over to the 2 year Training Course. Sir John ended with an appreciation of Miss Dickinson's work (the present Principal) and concluded by enquiring if anyone could think of a word to replace 'training' when it refers to the training of teachers.

Mr Haines (Chairman of Governors) then introduced Miss Freda Gwilliam, (Educational Advisor to the Ministry of Overseas Development) who began by saying she did not know who to pity more – herself for having to speak after Sir John, or the audience for having to listen to her after hearing Sir John. She mentioned the course for Overseas teachers held at Wall Hall in 1951. She had been talking in the Colonial Office of the needs of teachers in S.E.Asia, when Sir John enquired if half a College would be any use to her. From this suggestion came the most valuable course when 25 practising teachers from Hong Kong and Malaya spent one summer at

Wall Hall, joining in all the Students' activities.

The theme of her talk was the role of women in education in the future. We must not take for granted that education is free for all. The book 'Hope Deferred' describes how some of the great hopes of the present grandmothers have not been completely fulfilled. Miss Gwilliam would like to add a sequel called 'Hope Rising'. She had found this name when visiting Alicha on the banks of the Niger. Alicha has an enormous number of schools, all with the names of English public schools, until she came to one called Hope Rising Academy. Historically, women have always played a dual role, including that dying race of spinsters. In the past women were always concerned with the home and family in addition to helping on the land; she still plays a dual role and in rural communities this is so fully recognised that it is not even considered. People still fear the uniformity of education, although there is parity of the sexes. Every country must work out how best its skills and abilities may be harmonised. There is a need for the education of women and the education of public opinion that women can work on equal terms with men and still fulfil successfully their other role in the home.

Miss Gwilliam quoted from Plato on the equality of men and women. The community as a whole cannot do without the services of women: public opinion must accept this equality and the two roles of women must be in harmony. Men have the capacity for dispassionate planning – women deal successfully with the human side. She gave as an example of women's capabilities, Dame Evelyn Sharpe as the head of a great Ministry. Co-Educational Colleges and a mixed Staff are an enrichment, but there is a need for conscious awarement and preparation; proper preparation is absolutely necessary. There has been a Government conference and report on The Problems of Women at Work, but it has not been widely published or considered. At University and research level the quality of the work women can do is unequalled.

The audience was left with the consideration of their own future in dual roles and their personal approach to their own young people, especially in the 12–13 age range. This need not be a conflict, the difficulties can be overcome and can make more effective the job that lies ahead.

from left to right:
Sir John Newsom C.B.E.,
Miss Nancy Dickinson,
Miss Freda Gwilliam,
Miss J. McRoberts,
Alderman L. E. Haines.

CHAPTER 12

COLLEGE PRODUCTIONS

The production of "Comus" – 1949/50. Each student made her own costume.

The Dell – an Open Air Theatre was completed in 1952. It was frequently used by Students and Staff for their various productions of plays. It was originally an old chalk pit, also used during the 1939–945 Second World War for pistol and rifle shooting by the armed services and their allies.

"The School for Scandal" – 1947/1948. A College production – no name or date known.

COLLEGE PRODUCTIONS

The College Pantomime – 1954/56.

A Winters Tale – 1953.

"Antigone" – 1956.

"Twelfth Night" (in the Dell) – 1960.
Alison White plays Malvolio.
Photograph sent by Dianne Biggs (nee Ashcroft)
Dianne made the hedges.

Port Royal – 1980

The Maids – 1980.
(Jackie Brunning)

CHAPTER 13

THE MANSION AND GROUNDS

How the art studios used to look when used as a working farm

The cow byres.

The farmyard.

The original greenhouses utilised as Art studios.

Students preparing to work with children with disabilities involved in a "camping week" (possibly in the College grounds.)

THE MANSION AND GROUNDS

The Lodge - (entrance road to Wall Hall from Aldenham Village.) Pierpont Morgan used these houses for his senior staff.

Pictured in the winter and summer.

An English lesson in the grounds by the Lecturer (?Mr. Minnis).

CHAPTER 13

A VISIT BY PATRICK GORDON WALKER

A VISIT TO WALL HALL BY THE EDUCATION MINISTER IN 1968.

(Typed script from and Herts. Advertiser, February 16th. 1968.)

EDUCATION MINISTER HEARD LECTURE ON EDUCATION

A visitor to a class studying philosophy of education at Wall Hall College of Education, Aldenham, on Friday was Patrick Gordon Walker, Secretary of State for Education and Science.

Mr Walker looked into the class to listen to the lecturer, and hear the student teachers' views while making an informal visit to the college.

He arrived shortly before noon and was greeted by the Principal, Miss A. K. Davies. Others in the official party included the Chairman of Hertfordshire County Council, Mr C.C. Barker; the Chief Education Officer for Hertfordshire, Mr S. T. Broad; the Chairman of Hertfordshire Education Committee, Mr Bramwell Austin; and the Governor of the College Governors, Mr I. D. Bailey.

COCKTAIL PARTY – Mr Walker and the other visitors were entertained at a cocktail party before he made a brief tour of the College's latest lecture rooms and tutorial rooms, which were opened in 1966.

He was later entertained to lunch

Mr. Patrick Gordon Walker talks to Mrs.C. Oglesby and Mrs. B. MacFarlane in the embroidery class.

in the Staff Common Room and 41 guests sat down to a meal of melon cocktail, roast turkey, with all the trimmings, lemon meringue pie (or pineapple sponge) cheese and biscuits and coffee.

Wall Hall opened in 1945, has expanded considerably in recent years and today there are 650 students, of whom 150 are older men and women.

WALL HALL NOW TRAINS TEACHERS OF THE DEAF.

Visitors to the College soon begin to make inquiries about the history of the buildings and it is interesting to note that thirty years after opening as a teacher training establishment, the buildings now provided the setting for a training course for teachers of those with hearing handicaps.

The course opened in May 1975, and provided training for twelve to fifteen teachers each year. Students admitted to the course have included teachers from America, Nigeria and Ethiopia. Other teachers who qualify at Wall Hall attend to the educational needs of deaf children in Hertfordshire and other local authorities, including Wales.

Hertfordshire Education Authority has a fine reputation for its provision for hearing handicapped children, with assessment clinics, schools, units established throughout the County. Contrast the castellated facade of the training establishment at Wall Hall with the modern low building of the new Primary School for Deaf Children at Heathlands, St. Albans.

Teaching the deaf : A one year course for qualified teachers.

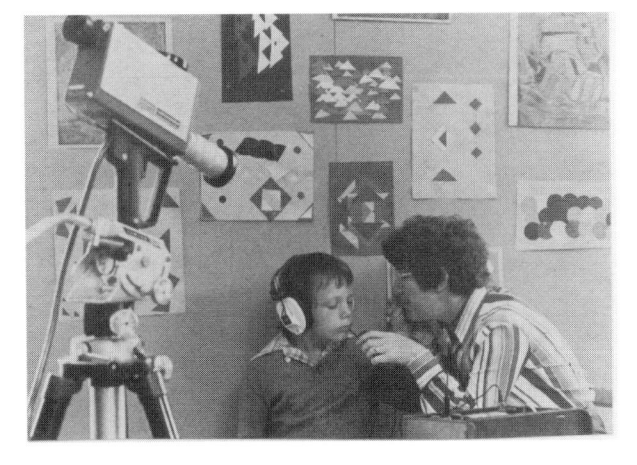

As one studies the changes, over many years, made to the property of Wall Hall, one cannot help but contrast them with the advances which brought about the improvements in the education of the hearing handicapped. When educators met in Milan (1880) for the International Congress on Deaf Education, a result of this conference, was the setting up in London for the oral (German) method of teaching and training.

In 1928, the invention of a pure tone audiometer proved that levels of deafness varied. By the time Hertfordshire County Council had taken an option on the purchase of Wall Hall in 1938, the use of modern batteries and reduction in the size of them had resulted in the operation of the one-piece hearing aid. Any wealthy deaf visitor to Wall Hall before then would have been encumbered with a heavy hearing aid and a separate battery compartment for storage in a pocket or handbag.

One of the first schools for those with partial hearing was opened at Tewin Water, near Welwyn in 1953, a venture which coincided with the development and greater use of transistors for hearing aids.

The emergency training course for teachers at Wall Hall had finished by this time and the college was established to run a two-year and later three-year courses. These courses were the forerunners of the present graduate training schemes which include work in nursery, infant, primary and secondary schools, and with the mentally handicapped, among others. The wood-panelled rooms which once accommodated important guests on, perhaps, shooting holidays, now echo to the sounds of electronic instruments measuring loudness, frequency and speech.

(Typed copy from a magazine article by H. Kernohan)

CHAPTER 15

COURSES RUNNING IN 1975

1. FULL TIME Three year: Certificate of Education. B.Ed. (ordinary)
One Year:-Postgraduate Certificate in Education, Diploma in Childhood Education, Certificate in Teaching Deaf and Partially Hearing Children.
One term:-Teaching in the Multi-Cultural School.

2. PART-TIME: In-Service B.Ed. 3/4 years.
In-Service Science in the Primary School. In-Service Mathematics in the Primary School. Many shorter courses.

WALL HALL COLLEGE – ACADEMIC STAFF
OCTOBER 1975.

Excluding the Principal, Deputy Principal and Librarian and counting two Staff on study leave as ? :-

Number of full-time staff : 62
Number of part-time staff : 9 = 4.1/10
   (full time equivalent.)
            Total : 66.1/10

(note: One full-time member of staff leaves in December and will not be replaced; further intake of B.Ed. part-time students in January.) Staff/Student ratio - 1.10 approximately.

Number of Principal Lecturers, excluding Principal and Deputy
   Principal: 16
Number of Senior Lecturers/Lecturers Grade 11
   (excluding Librarian): 50.1/10

All members of Staff have had teaching experience outside Colleges of Education; in schools, Further Education Colleges, Polytechnics or Universities.

Almost all of the staff have advanced qualifications over and above their original degrees or certificates. Many are at present engaged in further study. Within the next year or two 9 are likely to obtain Master's degrees, 4 Doctorates, 9 other degrees and diplomas. A further half dozen are embarking on courses of advanced study.

It has been College policy to encourage such study and the support of colleagues and the generous help of the County has made possible an impressive measure of staff development. The courses followed are highly relevant to the teaching within College. The staff is already well equipped for degree teaching and will be even more so shortly and for post-graduate work at various levels including advanced diplomas and a Master's degree in Education.

The present academic organisation is based on the *Academic Board* consisting of all full-time members of staff and 4 students. The Principal is Chairman and the Deputy Principal acts as Secretary.

All members of the teaching staff and heads of the administrative, non-teaching departments, constitute the Staff Meeting concerned with non-academic business.

WALL HALL COLLEGE – LINKS WITH NEIGHBOURING COMMUNITIES

The *Facilities* of the College are used in many ways:

By parties of *children* visiting the Rural Science unit, especially to see the farm animals. By school groups exploring the grounds, following College set up nature trails, studying architectural features, visiting the swimming pool, using the gymnasium, the dance and drama facilities, etc. In the academic year 1974-5 over 2,000 children visited the College for such purposes, coming from Hertfordshire and neighbouring areas. More could have been accommodated if facilities permitted.

By *teachers* using the reading centre, the library, the resources centre for their own purposes. A variety of professional bodies ask to hold meetings in the College; the Hertfordshire Association of English Teachers, the School Librarians and many others have recently met at Wall Hall. Schools borrow equipment, staging, costumes, audio-visual aids etc. Playing fields are used when available, by outside organisations. The library is open to the public for reference purposes.

The *coaches* and transit vans are hired by other organisations and the demand is greater than we can meet (see Paper on College Transport.)

The *swimming pool* is used by a large number of families from Radlett, Watford, etc., during the summer vacation and has provided many young children with the opportunity to learn to swim.

A wide range of organisations, including local Educational Institutions such as Oaklands College of Agriculture, Cassio College, use the College for *residential conferences.* In spite of limited accommodation and catering problems it is possible to make some term-time lettings at the week-end for local Teachers' Conferences and for other groups. A party of teachers is at present spending considerable time at week-ends here in building outdoor kilns to test theories about Roman pottery-making techniques.

Links with local schools are extensive. Teaching practice is confined to certain agreed areas including the immediate locality, Watford, Hemel Hempstead, Berkamsted, Tring, Boreham Wood, Rickmansworth, Maple Cross, parts of Stevenage, St. Albans and Welwyn. For courses associated with training teachers of the deaf, and Mentally Handicapped and Nursery age children a wider area can be used since local Colleges are not in competition in offering these specialisms. Well over 100 Hertfordshire schools are regularly used for teaching practice and visits. Within a ten mile radius 105 schools are closely associated with the College and many others are contacted, though less frequently.

The College has a *Nursery School* for local children: 20 attending in the morning from Garston and 20 in the afternoon from Radlett. These include severely disadvantaged and handicapped children. A service is thus provided for the community as well as giving students the opportunity of consistent observation of children. Parents serve on the sub-committee responsible for the Nursery School and contribute with much generosity to the provision of facilities both financially and by practical activities such as constructing the sand pit.

The establishment of the in-service B.Ed. and the expansion of in-service courses has strengthened links with local schools. Some

165 teachers are at present attending wall Hall weekly for study purposes and thus get to know the staff and the resources of the College very well. College tutors, of course, frequently visit schools to see students and to take classes themselves. They serve on Teachers' Centre Committees, on the new Divisional Committees concerned with the induction year programme and the provision of in-service courses, on the Further Education in-service training committee; on CNAA visiting parties and advisory panels. Members of staff serve as external examiners for B.Ed. and Certificate in Education in London, Leeds, etc. they are examiners for C.S.E., 'O' and 'A' levels.

Staff and students are associated with *local activities* such as the Watford Theatre in Education, the Immigrants' Centre, the Cassio College based Social Education Project. Students work in a voluntary capacity with play centres, youth clubs, holiday play groups, on gypsy sites, with handicapped children, with local Cub Scouts, Brownies, Guides, Sunday Schools, drama and art clubs, etc. The Students' Union has organised Christmas parties for local children and is one of the sponsors of the Watford Rag, raising large sums for charity. Students use the facilities of the Hertsmere Centre, the gymnastics coaching at George Stephenson College, the Sailing sessions at Cheshunt, Aldenham and Rickmansworth. Staff and students are closely associated with Cuffley Camp. Going a little further afield, use has been made of teaching or performance opportunities at the Art of Movement Studio (Weybridge) the London School of Contemporary dance, various Arts Centres, theatres and concert halls in London.

Though placed in a particularly attractive rural area, students for the most part have some experience of teaching in town schools; Watford, Hemel Hempstead, etc. opportunities are taken to visit areas with particular urban problems, e.g Brent, the East End of London, with which the College, through its tutors, has many links. While about one-third of the student population at present comes from the County, or nearby, there can be no guarantee that students will spend their teaching lives in any one kind of environment and the attempt is, therefore, made to give a broad range of experience.

The College has a policy of releasing students, when practicable, to accompany *school parties* on field weeks and day visits when additional adult help is required. This is, of course, a valuable experience for students preparing to teach as well as a means of offering practical assistance to the schools.

WALL HALL COLLEGE – ACCOMODATION SCHEDULE.

Teaching Space

Teaching rooms, including Lecture Rooms and Practical Rooms.

Location No: of rooms Area (square feet.)

Mansion	12	4,245
Central Block	2	680
Central Hall	1	3,486
Music Wing	2	1,266
Educational Centre	6	5,110
Gymnasium	1	2,850
Dance and Drama Block	1	1,024
Lab. Block	6	4,410
Rural Science	1	260
Studio Block		4,300
Chiltern Consortium & Wall Hall CCTV		2,140
		29,771
Tutorial Rooms		
Mansion	6	752
Central Block	2	100
Music Wing	4	340
Education Centre	16	2,090
Gymnasium	1	80
Dance and Drama Block	4	900
Lab. Block	8	770
Rural Science	1	80
Studio Block	7	680
		5,792

Study Space and Teaching Practice Preparation Rooms.

Library (excluding Seminar Room)	7,630
Resources centre (including Seminar room)	1,350

TRANSPORT

1. *Personnel*
   1 Transport officer
   6 Drivers

2. *Vehicles*
   All College vehicles are Ford diesel engines chassis with production-line bodies. The vehicle fleet consists of:
   5 x 45 seater coaches
   2 x 15 seater Transit buses
   1 x Transit van for administrative purposes
   College has its own diesel fuel tanks situated next to the transport Office and drivers' rest room adjacent to garaging for five of the eight vehicles.

3. *College use*
   Vehicles are used for:
   3.1 Transporting students to and from Lodgings
   3.2 Transporting students to and from teaching practice schools, observation visits etc.
   3.3 Environmental studies
   3.4 Field Week Studies
   3.5 Music and Dramatic tours on the Continent
   3.6 Transporting Nursery Class children to and from collecting areas at Garston and Radlett
   3.7 Transporting Daily Ladies in Catering and Domestic duties morning and afternoon from the Garston area.

(*left*) The College Bus in the Swansea area – a students' field trip in 1966.
(*right*) The Thatched Barn on the A1 at Borehamwood, students being taken for swimming in 1965

Photographs sent by Miss Margaret Smeaton.

4. *Hertfordshire County Council Use*
   During the year 1974–1975 College coaches were used by the County council on the following details:
   4.1 Transporting the County Youth Orchestra and Choir within the United Kingdom — 6,411 miles
   4.2 Transporting Foreign students for the County Education Department including:

International Summer School	747 miles
German Teachers	564 miles
Head Teachers	50 miles
Foreign teachers	827 miles

   4.3 Schools and Adult Education centres were transported on studies on repayment to the County — 3,644 miles
   4.4 School children were transported to College for Rural Science Studies, Movement and Drama classes etc. with College students — 2,130 miles
   4.5 Foreign tours were undertaken on repayment to County for:

Balls Park French Language Department Field Week to France	602 miles
Watford College of Further Education, tour of Western Vineyards	1,262 miles
Herts. County Council Youth Choir tour to Strasbourg	4,622 miles
Herts. County Council Youth Orchestra tour to France	3,666 miles

STUDY SPACE AND TEACHING PRACTICE PREPARATION ROOMS

	Area (Sq. Ft.)
Reading Workshop	1090
Education Centre – Day Study	600
Dance and Drama Block – Study	370
Workshop space	770
Computer Link Room	130
	2960

Student Common Rooms

Mansion (Old Common Room in Prefab., also used as coffee and sandwich room.)	1050
Central Block	390
	1440

Education Centre
   (Shared with Buttery – see under Dining Rooms)
   Staff Common Room – Mansion   1200

Students' Union
   Council Room and Office (shared with Bank)   200

Kitchens
Central Block Main Kitchen	1560
Education Centre Buttery Kitchen	440
Common Room 1 Snack Kitchen	130
Common Room 11 Snack Kitchen	70
Outside food store and deep freeze	400
Cold store (cubic capacity 455 Cubic feet)	70
	2670

Dining rooms
Central Block – Students Dining Room	2460
Staff Dining Room	450
Common Room 11 – see above	660

Education Centre – Buttery shared with Common Room
                                                          1150
                                                        4720

Administration
MANSION – Principal's Office and Study	270
Deputy Principal's Office and Study	130
Registrar's Office	140
Principal's Secretary's Office	110
Domestic Bursar's Office and Store	200

CENTRAL BLOCK – General Office	240
Bursar's Office	90
Assistant Domestic Bursar's Office	90
Caterer's Office	55

EDUCATION CENTRE – Teaching Practice Organiser's Office
                                                           100
                                                          1425

General Teaching Facilities

THE LIBRARY The Library is housed in a new building opened in October 1971, embracing an area of 7,630 feet. Seating is provided for 128 readers. The main book collection and administrative offices are sited downstairs and upstairs are the children's book collection, the periodical room, the Library seminar room, (also used for Educational Technology classes) and the resource centre.

Hours of opening have recently been extended and Library service is now available seven days a week as follows :-

Monday & Tuesday	8.45 a.m. – 9.00 p.m.
Wednesday & Thursday	8.45 a.m. – 7.00 p.m.
Friday	8.45 a.m. – 5.30 p.m.
Saturday	9.00 a.m. – 2.00 p.m.
Sunday	3.00 p.m. – 8.00 p.m.

A total of 63¾ hours per week.

The present book stock is in excess of 45,000 volumes, with 220 periodicals taken, plus a considerable collection of non-book items in the Resource Centre. Other book collections are located in small departmental libraries, amounting to over 1,000 volumes. A photocopier and microfilm reader are sited in the Library building. External link services via the Hertfordshire County Library and through the Hertfordshire Technical Information Service, and a postal loan service through the British Library Lending Division and the Cambridge Institute of Education.

Almost all the material housed in the library is available for loan, with the exception of certain reference books and books temporarily reserved. All new students are given instructions in library use, and follow-up facilities in the form of video tapes and slide tape programmes are provided for individual use. A printed Library and Resource Centre Guide is distributed to all students. The Librarian is on the Academic Staff and offers or contributes to courses in Learning resources and Information Retrieval as part of the in-service degree programme, and to the Induction to Study course on the full-time B.Ed. course.

The staff under the tutor-librarian consists of two professionally qualified librarians, 3 full-time clerical assistants and 1½ term-time clerical assistants. A sum of £10,000 is allocated in the present financial year for the purchase of books, for binding and for journals.

The Resource Centre
The Resource centre occupies part of the Library building and in conjunction with the Wall Hall television Unit, provides a wide range of materials and services for staff and students. A Senior Lecturer in Educational Technology is in overall charge of the Resource centre and television unit. He is responsible for the organisation and introductory courses in educational technology for full-time students and also for the Educational Technology option which forms part of the In-service B.Ed. degree.

The department has a wide range of equipment for use by all college departments and its sound recording and reprographic facilities are in heavy demand by both students and staff.

A major role of the Resources Centre is to provide learning materials (wall charts, film strips and slides, audio-tapes etc.) for use by students in schools. In addition to these materials, the department stocks a variety of audio visual items, including a substantial number of Open University audio tapes, which students may borrow for private study in connection with their academic courses in College.

The resource centre has its own secretarial and technical staff.

The Wall Hall Television Unit.
This unit has its own equipment and a television studio for making recordings on the College site. A portable camera and video tape recorder allow programmes to be made in schools and later replayed to students in College.

The unit is responsible for recording all television broadcasts required by other departments and offers replay facilities in a number of locations on the College site.

The unit has its own full-time camera operator/technician.

The Chiltern Consortium.
This television production unit is sited at Wall Hall and serves the following Colleges – Bedford College of Education, Bedford College of Physical Education, Newland Park, Putteridge Bury and Wall Hall Colleges of Education and the Advisory service of the Brent Local Education Authority. As a constituent member, this College is able to draw on video tape, slide tape or other material

commissioned by any of the members and has access to the products of other Consortia, as well as a link with the Hertfordshire Educational Television Unit at Goldings, Hertford. The Consortium is licensed by the Open University to reproduce its programmes.

The team consists of a Director, Engineer, Production Manager, Librarian, Clerk of Graphics and Photography Specialist, with seconded staff, this year a School teacher. The current loan catalogue lists about 400 items.

Art

The studio and workshop areas consist of a separate pottery, and, nearby, a series of rooms at ground level forming an 'L' shape, linked with inter-communicating doors. This arrangement facilitates an inter-disciplinary approach, enabling students to move freely between areas as the need arises, while offering at the same time well equipped specialist studio workshops.

There are 7 tutorial rooms in the department. The painting area, studio 1 and studio 2 provide about 1,800 square feet, with a workshop area of 170 square feet. A range of painting media and equipment, including compressor and spray-gun is provided.

The printmaking area, of approaching 800 square feet, includes screen-printing equipment, mercury vapour lamp, multisize screen stretcher, vacuum cabinet, litho press, 'Albion' press, print drying racks, a range of small equipment, 3 sinks and large bins.

The textile area consists of 3 studios totalling nearly 1,800 square feet. This includes equipment for dyeing, printing, spinning, weaving, fabric construction, embroidery and dress. There are 19 sewing machines (electric and manual) and a knitting machine, table and floor looms, boilers and a range of small equipment.

The ceramics studio is approximately 840 square feet and a sculpture studio approximately 1,080 square feet. the first is equipped with 'cromatic' electric kilns, (8 cubic feet each) 1 'Catterson Smith' electric kiln (4 cubic feet) 1 'Hertfordshire' electric kiln (2 cubic feet) 1 gas kiln (5 cubic feet) 5 electric pottery wheels, 1 kick wheel, 1 claymixer, 1 pug mill. Glaze spraying equipment, an extractor cabinet, a range of workbenches, storage provision and a damp cupboard are provided.

In the sculpture studio, the following are available – oxyacetylene welding and cutting equipment, brazing equipment, plunging router, miscellaneous power and hand tools. There are facilities for work in plastic and fibre glass.

The department has its own darkroom with photographic equipment, including still cameras, 8 mm cine camera, 2 enlargers, print drier and it has access to the College resource centre facilities and equipment, as well as to the Wall Hall and Chiltern Consortium television equipment and resources. The department is equipped with an epidiascope, slide and film projector. Most of the studios and one of the tutorial rooms can be blacked out.

There are 7 tutorial rooms of approximately 100 square feet each; 7 store rooms and storage areas of approximately 1,000 square feet.

The reference material includes 3,600 slides, with access to the 30,000 slide collection at Watford School of Art.

Staffing – a full time technician is attached to the department.

Drama

Work in Drama is very closely associated with that of the English department and rooms may be used by either. The purpose built studio in the Dance/Drama block (over 1,000 square feet) contains a full range of lighting and sound equipment, with 2 adjacent workshops equipped for Art and Craft work as well as the construction of scenery and properties. These are used both by the students and parties of children from neighbouring schools on working visits to the College. There is a seminar room (used also as a dressing room) and a large stage wardrobe. There are several tutorial rooms for the use of the Drama staff in the building. Supplementary equipment includes portable tape recorders, an overhead projector, art and craft material. The main Assembly Hall of the College is also used for Drama. This is well equipped with stage lighting and movable staging. An open-air theatre in the grounds is an additional facility.

Staffing – a full-time (term-time) assistant is shared with the English Department.

Education

The education centre provides 4 lecture rooms (each about 550 square feet) and the use of the lecture theatre, (1,500 square feet) for lectures and seminars in the Education Department. Most of the Education staff have tutorial rooms in the building (using 14 rooms.) The Nursery School is sited in the building, with the reading centre and the computer terminal. In the Mansion, 4 lecture rooms (of about 400 square feet each) are used for departmental lectures and seminars. Equipment includes a 16mm film projector, strip projectors, language masters, overhead projector, a duplicator, with access to other equipment in the Reading Centre, Resources Centre and television facilities.

Staff – the department has its own office with 1 senior secretary and 2 part-time clerical assistants.

English

Accomodation is to some extent shared with Drama and, in addition, 4 lecture rooms are available in the Mansion (570 square feet, 370 square feet, 220 square feet) 5 tutorial rooms are provided for the department. It is supplied with record player, tape recorders, 8 mm cine cameras, an overhead projector, radios. Much use is made of the television facilities of the College.

Staffing – the department shares a clerical assistant with drama.

Geography

The area at present allocated to this field of study consists of 2 laboratories (area: 570 square feet and 500 square feet) with 3 tutorial rooms, a fully equipped photographic dark room and a storeroom which houses a comprehensive range of survey equipment. The laboratories have been designed to fulfil the dual purpose of lecture/seminar and practical rooms in which the students can carry out analytical and experimental work in connection with the lecture courses and field studies. In these laboratories is stored an extensive collection and range of equipment used to illustrate the professional courses. Some of this material is loaned to students for use in schools. Additional items include an 8" telescope, meterological and a wide range of reprographic and audio-visual equipment.

Staffing – a cartographer and a clerical assistant (part-time.)

History

The department has 3 lecture rooms in the Mansion (255 square feet) 360 square feet and 270 square feet) with 3 tutorial rooms. Available equipment includes three slide projectors, an overhead projector, an epidiascope, a record player, three tape recorders, a duplicator, a typewriter and a 35 mm camera. The department holds a large collection of teaching materials, a journal and pamphlet collection, historical maps and documents and a collection of archaeologocal material. Students benefit from these facilities not only for academic purposes but through the loan of a wide range of audio visual and documentary material for use on teaching practice. There is a display and cupboard space on the landing adjoining the department in addition to that available in the lecture and tutorial rooms. Intensive use is made of this space for the display of exhibition material which has been drawn on several occasions from collections of national importance.

Staffing – a clerical assistant.

Mathematics

2 lecture rooms (640 square feet and 670 square feet) in the Education Centre are used for Mathematics teaching, with a computer room adjacent, and computer link with the Hatfield Polytechnic computer. 4 tutorial rooms are provided in the Education Centre. New teaching areas for the department are provided in the proposed new building. The department is well supplied with workbenches, storage space and has an overhead projector, duplicator, calculators, Olivetti desk top computer, computer terminal and a considerable amount of small items of mathematicsal equipment. Considerable use is made of CCTV in terms of TV schools programmes.

Staffing – 1 part-time technical assistant.

Movement

The department works mainly in the gymnasium (2,850 square feet) the central hall (1,900 square feet) with occasional use of the Dance/Drama studio (1,024 square feet.) One tutorial room is provided for the department in the gymnasium building and 2 others elsewhere. Games provision includes 5 tennis courts, a hockey pitch, a football field, a heated open-air swimming pool. Gymnastic apparatus includes vaulting and climbing equipment, athletics equipment, small games equipment. The department has 2 Sony and 5 Phillips portable tape recorders, 1 cabinet tape recorder and record player, other recording apparatus and has access to the Chiltern Consortium television, the audio-visual aids of the Resources Centre and the lighting facilities of the Dance/Drama studio.

150 WALL HALL FROM FARMHOUSE TO UNIVERSITY

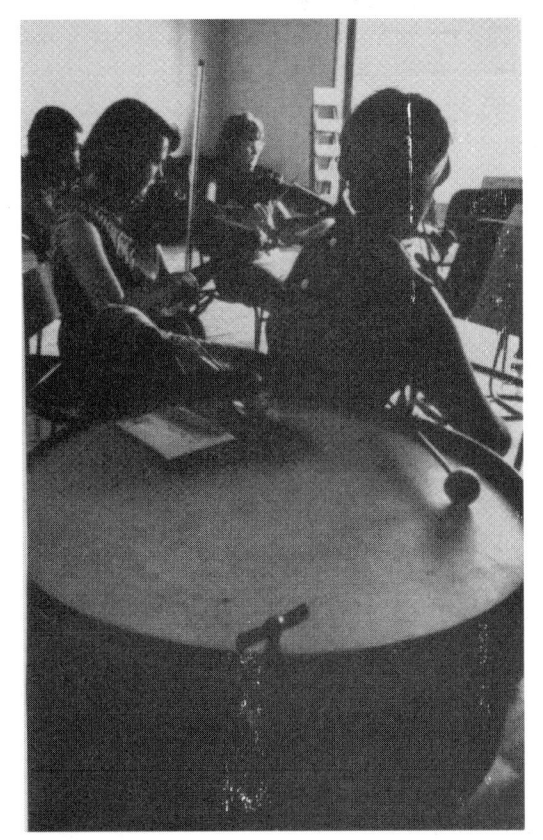

Practising in the
Dance Studio.

Music students
preparing for an
informal concert.

Pictures from a Wall Hall
Prospectus.

Music
The department is housed in the specially built Music Wing, consisting of a large recital room (840 square feet) and a small lecture room (nearly 300 square feet) with 4 tutorial rooms and 8 practice rooms. Storage is provided for instruments, about 2,000 records, 1,000 scores, sheets of music, etc. the extensive range of equipment includes an electronic organ, spinnet, 2 grand pianos, 12 upright pianos, 6 'pianets' with double sets of headphones for supervised practice, recorders, percussion instruments, classical guitars, violins, violas, cellos, flutes, clarinets, trumpets, horns, timpani, and others. The department is supplied with an E.M.S. VCS3 synthesiser, with keyboard and sequences; 6 tape recorders and 2 stereo record playback systems and 4 extra decks, with headphones for private listening.

Instrumental teaching is provided in piano and other instruments by 5 part-time teachers. The proximity of the Watford School of Music make additional help readily available.

Religious Education
The department is housed in the Mansion, with the use of 1 lecture room (about 500 square feet) and 2 tutorial rooms. It is provided with a slide/film strip projector, a tape recorder, an overhead projector, display units, a typewriter. There is an extensive collection of reference books, pamphlets, maps, charts, pictures, 300 slides, 20 audio tapes, 6 video tapes etc.

Sociology
The department uses 1 lecture room in the Education Department and has 2 tutorial rooms.

The Sciences
Biology, Biogeography and curriculum courses in Health Education and Physical Sciences are housed in the Geography/Science block using 3 laboratories (500 square feet, 700 square feet, 780 square feet) with 1 laboratory (1,200 square feet) and a small animal room (200 square feet) in the adjacent Holbrook building. There are 5 tutorial rooms and a Prep. room. Rural Science/Applied Biology occupies a separate building consisting of a laboratory (270 square feet) and tutorial room with associated dairy, equipment sheds, animal quarters and 2 greenhouses (in addition to the small green-

house associated with the Biology laboratories.) A new environmental greenhouse has been erected and equipment has been ordered which will permit the simulation of a variety of differing environments in which native and exotic plants will be grown under controlled conditions. There are 2 paddocks (1 acre and ? acre) for grazing by the larger animals and an area of garden plots which the students cultivate as part of their course work. Extensive use is made of the College grounds and neighbouring farmland for experiments on the use of fertilizers, observation on the occurence and control of horticultural pests and diseases and farming operations.

Ancillary staff is provided by 2 technicians, one associated particularly with animals husbandry (mainly goats, cows, breeding sow, rabbits and bees) and the other a scientific technician and assistant.

General Amenities.
Staff Common Room – 2 are provided in the Mansion.

Student Common Rooms – are distributed in the hostels (5) general building (1) with limited use as common rooms of the Buttery and the hut known as the Old Common Room. The Staff/Student bar is in the central building common room. Additional common room and Students' Union Office facilities are proposed in the new building.

A book-shop, open daily, is at the back of the Old Common Room and a stationery shop, open on a similar basis, is in the Mansion. The local branch of Westminster Bank makes its facilities available in a bank sub-branch, functioning in the College once a week.

The Central Hall (1,900 square feet) is used as a teaching area (particularly for Movement and Drama) and as a place of assembly for Student Union and other large meetings or lectures, for concerts, dances, badminton and a multiplicity of purposes.

WALL HALL COLLEGE ACADEMIC LINKS WITH OTHER ORGANISATIONS.

The College is associated with the Cambridge Institute for:

The 3 year certificate in Education
The 1 year Postgraduate Certificate in Education
The 1 year Diploma in Early Childhood Education
The 1 year Certificate in Teaching of the Deaf and Partially Hearing.
The 1 term course on Teaching in the Multi-Cultural School
Various short part-time courses.

with the *University of Cambridge* for:
4th. year B.Ed. with the University of East Anglia for:
4th. year B.Ed.

with the *Council of National Academic Awards* for:
The part-time in-service B.Ed.
The full-time 3 year B.Ed. and 4th. year B.Ed. with Honours.

Negotiations are proceeding with the CNAA for validation of all courses offered by the College (other than very short part-time courses) including the new B.A.(Ed.) degree at present with the Regional Advisory Council.

The part-time in-service B.Ed. is run jointly with Balls Park College, the Hatfield Polytechnic and Putteridge Bury College, Luton.

The new full-time B.Ed. is run in association with Balls Park and Hockerill Colleges, following common syllabuses and with academic powers in respect of the degree delegated by the individual Academic Boards to the inter-collegiate Academic Committee.

The *Chiltern Consortium* is an Educational television production unit working in the field of initial and in-service training of teachers. It is based at Wall Hall College. The costs are

4 October 1973 – A visit to Wall Hall by the Minister of Education, Thailand, especially interested in the C.C.T.V. Chiltern Consortium work. Miss Kay Davies on the left, is standing with the Minister and Alan George (C.C.T.V.) and a Thai representative.

July 1979 – From left to right:
Nan Hill, (Physical Education tutor) Kay Roberts, (Domestic Bursar) Kay Davies (Principal) and the mother of Keiko Naksugy.

Photographs sent by Miss A.K.Davies.

shared by Hertfordshire (relating to Wall Hall,) Bedfordshire (Bedford College of Education, Bedford College of Physical Education and Putteridge Bury College of Education) Buckinghamshire, (Newland Park College of Education) and Brent (the L.E.A. advisory team.) The services of the unit are in considerable demand and many copies of video tapes have been sold in this country and abroad. Various national bodies, e.g. Schools Council, have commissioned work.

Apart from the in-service B.Ed. connection, the College is associated with the Hatfield Polytechnic through the computer service and is at present investigating closer link with the library through the adoption of common cataloguing procedures. There has been co-operation in discussing the Diploma of Higher Education and it is envisaged that some kind of association in academic planning will be established when the new institution comes into being, after the merging of the two Colleges of Education.

The College Library provides access for staff and students to many other academic libraries, including those in London.

This material has been typed from documents held in the Hertfordshire County Records at Hertford.

CHAPTER 16.

WALL HALL AFTER 40 YEARS

KAY DAVIES - PRINCIPAL (1966-1981)

Forty years may now seem and obvious date for a special celebration of the founding of an institution, but there is the advantage that there are still active people about who took part in the original opening ceremony and remember it well.

By the time I came in 1966, succeeding Miss Dickinson, there were still on the Staff, original founding members. They had already seen the College lose its 'Emergency' College status and the change in recruiting from 'mature' entrants, following a special shortened course, to the normal 18 year old entry following a two year teacher training course just changed to three years. Numbers had expanded to about 400 and the College was entering a new phase as a College of Education, subsequently to be renamed a College of Higher Education. A period of rapid expansion was dawning to meet the needs of the school population explosion. A range of new buildings had been added, the Education Centre was almost ready and a host of new Staff appointments had to be made - all heady stuff, though unsettling to those who liked a quiet life.

My first shock came when the LEA announced that further expansion was on the way and I was asked to start planning in terms of 1,000 students. We never reached beyond 730 at Wall Hall, though after the amalgamation with Balls Park in 1976, the joint College student numbers exceeded 1,000. For the whole of my time as Principal there was a dizzying succession of changes with accompanying traumas and looking back I wonder that the Staff, academic, administrative and domestic, remained so positive and supportive.

We acquired an impressive fleet of navy blue coaches to take Students to schools and on enterprising study tours. The gardeners, with declining numbers, became ever more mechanized and yet managed to maintain well kept and attractively varied gardens. Formal meals for Students and Staff gave way under the pressure of numbers to cafeteria like arrangements, with a gain in speed and economy, but a loss of social graces. The entry of men students and increase in the number of men Staff added a welcome dimension. I well remember the way the first men Students moved about in a protective group for their first week amidst so many women! Reduction of the age of majority made possible a considerable relaxation of residence requirements, with no little relief to Wardens and the Principal who were no longer obliged to take some sort of midnight action to trace a late returning Student.

Courses in the College changed with a bewildering rapidity, new ones being instituted, among them sociology, biogeography, sculpture, MENCAP, the course for teachers of the hearing impaired, a post graduate programme. Wall Hall had always made a point of admitting mature Students for initial teacher training; now there was a vast increase, in the late 70's in the provision of in-service courses leading to a degree and higher degree work and to non-vocational study.

The introduction of the B.Ed. followed by the phasing out of the old Certificate course presented us with great problems. The University of Cambridge would admit Students to degrees only on the basis of a resident 4th year within the University. During the protracted initial negotiations we enjoyed an interim arrangement with London University, based in our own College. For a while our Students moved on to Cambridge (usually to either Homerton or Wolfson Colleges) for the final part of the degree course. Later we decided to seek degree validation through the Council for National Academic Awards and the teacher training and arts degrees were then entirely College based. This last development plunged the Staff into an apparently endless succession of course board meetings for syllabus construction followed by traumas of validation meetings with CNAA and full scale reviews of virtually all aspects of College activity. For a while we were closely associated with Balls Park and Hockerill Colleges in a joint degree programme and with the Hatfield Polytechnic for an in-service degree. These joint enterprises provided the interest and stimulus of visiting other Colleges and sent travelling expenses soaring, to the alarm of those responsible for finance.

The later 70's saw the beginning and acceleration of the dramatic cut-back in Student numbers, introducing a different kind of uncertainty, when the very survival of the College could not be assumed. Building plans were suspended (the Drama block and Library were through just in time.) A very difficult period came when after much anguish on all sides, Balls Park College was merged with Wall Hall, operating for some two years on both sites. The merger brought the enlivening stimulus of new Staff, new administrative procedures and new courses (French, Secondary teacher training for example.) A general re-organisation was necessary with new committee structures and with an Academic Board taking the place of the old Staff meeting. There was a much larger element of Student participation in the devising of academic and other policies through membership of the Governing Body and Academic Board. The management of the Student bar was the responsibility of a more forceful and sometimes more militant Student Union.

No sooner were we beginning to feel that these changes were being assimilated than the really telling financial cuts began, leading to many early Staff retirements (happily on Crombie terms), and forced economies in all directions. The threat of absorption within the Hatfield Polytechnic was an ever present anxiety and the College, by now named the Hertfordshire College of Higher Education, was very much on the defensive. Its survival owed a great deal to Staff and Student support, the strong backing of a Governing body and of the wider community of local schools and the vigorous Old Student Association.

I wish that I could end this note with the assumption that a period of peace and consolidation will follow the particularly traumatic last fifteen years, but it does not appear that there is yet any reasonable prospect of quiet stability. Only on retiring in 1981 did I realise just how hectic the previous ten years had been and the adjustment to a less frenetic pace of living took a little time - after the first prolonged holiday feeling had evaporated it seemed odd to be free to structure the day as I wished and I sometimes found this difficult to manage without the shepherding and guiding of good secretaries and administrators. I kept double booking myself with engagements! However, this phase passed and I now enjoy enormously the leisure to entertain and visit friends, to travel and to garden, let alone read, which was virtually impossible before. At the same time I value the continuing links I have with Higher Education and Teacher Training, without the pressures and strains of my previous responsibilities. Retirement has much to recommend it! It is particulary a pleasure to meet former Staff and Students, so many of whom speak with great warmth and appreciation of their association with the College and recall people and events, plays and concerts and the splendid parties of past days. In spite of all the alarms and vicissitudes so much was achieved and we can take a legitimate pride in the College's contribution to Higher Education and Teacher Training.

MARGARET DAVIES – ART TUTOR.

It is hard to believe that it is forty years since the first days at Wall Hall, when eleven Staff and just under 100 students saw the inauguration of an innovative, bold and imaginative scheme for the training of teachers. The war was nearly over and there was a great need for more teachers in the profession. All the initial members of staff had been invited by the then Board of Education to get this first Women's Emergency Training College established and, as you can imagine, one of the strengths of a comparitively small Staff (each of whom respected everybody else's knowledge and experience in her own field) was the inevitability and pleasure of informal conversations and discussions in which we became aware of much of the basic knowledge and the underlying principles which other people thought important in their particular interest or discipline. I know that as I learnt something of the methods used in teaching of reading and in the encouragement of conversation and the enjoyment of words and in the use of numbers, I became increasingly aware of how much the visual arts and their allied skills, including handwriting, could and should contribute towards making the classroom environment and the equipment the children used, something that could be of lasting value to them and which could make the school a more stimulating and congenial place for everyone in it. We certainly had to use our wits about the provision of materials of all kinds in those immediate post-war years.

All the Students except two, were in their twenties and thirties, as indeed were most of the Staff and because of the way in which the war had broken or interrupted so many lives there was a strong feeling in the air that here was an opportunity for a new beginning,

Miss Margaret Davies, with her beloved corgi "Ben" and Students.

for being part of a kind of renaissance, however humble. A tremendous amount of work of all kinds was accomplished in that one year. We worked straight through to the following May with only a fortnight's break in August and a week in November and at Christmas. As everyone was in residence the evenings were often used for recitals, visits from outside lecturers and so on; I remember that towards the end of the course I gave a series of talks on European painting, illustrated by monochrome slides borrowed from the Courtauld Institute, as colour transparencies as we know them had not appeared on the scene.

Like everybody else I have lasting memories of the impact the place itself made on us: the solidity of the Mansion, the plants and vines and peaches still in the greenhouses, the beauty and serenity of the gardens... a rose garden and Michaelmas daisy garden where there are now tennis courts... the cowslip and daffodil fields, the woodlands and farmlands. Blackbirds farm had some magnificent Percheron horses, who after their day's work were let loose to roll *(top)* Wall Hall Mansion in the Springtime. *(bottom)* The Mansion in late Autumn. Photographs by Joan Beagle.

and gallop in the fields where the footpath goes down to the river, the youngsters sooty dark and the older ones silvery grey and white in colour. Berrygrove was a larch wood, full of bluebells and willow herb and birdsong, no thought of a motorway or of an intersection bearing its name.

There was little petrol to be had and there were only two of three cars amongst us. We cycled or walked up and down to Otterspool and into Radlett or Watford to do our shopping. I used to cycle to Letchmore Heath. In the early days the Studio was at Otterspool, an elegant and inspirational setting. The Conservatory was still standing and three or four students could work there, with two camellia trees for company. I then lived down there and I remember so many pale sunny mornings, when on the far side of the river the herd of cows was just visible above the lingering low-lying mist and against the shadowy willows, for all the world like a neat monochrome Chinese painting, with a more sharply defined heron silent and still on the bank. The garden provided a wealth of material for painting and pattern making of all kinds, done out of doors or in the Studio. I can still see in my mind's eye some very lovely paintings, mostly in sepia, which the Main Course group made of the garden in Winter. My corgi, Ben, enjoyed a good life there too. He usually attached himself to the Student of his choice for the morning or afternoon and sat or slept by her side.

I have so many happy memories of the schools which hosted us for teaching practice and of their kindness and hospitality. One in particular, I shall never forget. Much later on in the College's life, on a warm afternoon in early Summer I went into this village infant school where a large class of children was working very quietly and diligently at paintings and construction of one kind or another. At this time Davy Crockett was the reigning folk hero and practically every small boy was wearing, with varying degrees of panache, his Davy Crockett hat, made at home from all kinds of bits of fur and fur fabric, with the obligatory tail comfortably lodged against the owner's neck. Their enlightened Headmistress allowed this as an 'afternoon only' privilege!

In 1945 I was seconded from the Cambridge and County High School for Girls for two years but Wall Hall became a permanent College and I stayed there until 1969! This sounds a long time to be in one place, but as no two years were ever remotely the same, with numbers growing, different groups of Students (who covered a wide range in age and previous experience and included a party of Malay and Chinese Students from the Far East) coming for longer and shorter courses, old buildings being converted and new ones going up all over the Estate, there was never any feeling of standing still.

ELIZABETH HAIGH - ENGLISH TUTOR.

In 1952 I joined the Staff of the small College for Women in the gracious country Mansion of Wall Hall, the first non-resident full-time Lecturer to be appointed. I found a lively, enterprising community and at once enjoyed working with gifted, enthusiastic colleagues, and friendly eager students. Memories crowd in: rehearsing in The Dell with spray guns to keep the gnats at bay; becoming involved in unexpected experiences such as painting, singing or dancing on 'Special Feature Days'; taking part in and producing astonishing entertainments when Christmas spirit spread through the College; gazing with fresh eyes at the College grounds when a far-Eastern student was upset at the mowing of the star-like daisies, or an African girl marvelled when people walked on water in the frost of mid-winter. I realise how versatile we all became in such a small community, how friendly we were, how well we came to know and appreciate each other.

Great days lay ahead in the years of expansion. It was wonderful to have a better Library and adaptable Hall, a Gymnasium, a Dance/Drama Studio, television equipment and still more wonderful, to welcome men staff and students, mature students, graduates and specialists. There was always fresh interest and excitement as the years flew by. There were many, many meetings to establish and replan courses with Staff from Universities and other Colleges, with colleagues at Wall Hall, with teachers, with students and with children. I also had the privilege of being the first staff representative on the Board of Governors. My job inevitably became more concerned with organisation and administration, but always at the heart of the matter was tutoring students who were seeking to equip themselves for the adventure of teaching. Everywhere the people I worked with enabled me to feel that I was always learning as well as teaching.

HAZEL WILKINSON - EDUCATION TUTOR

When I became a student in 1954, the College was quite small, about 120 students altogether, that is fifty in each of the two years and twenty more mature students who did a one year course. None of the new buildings were erected at that time. Art took place in Otterspool, craft and pottery classes were held in the greenhouses. Almost all students lived in and I was lucky enough to spend my second year in the farm-house which had just been vacated by the farmer and his family. The present art block and farm hostels were still as the farmer and his cows had left them.

CHAPTER 17.

INTERIOR PHOTOGRAPHS OF THE MANSION

The Main Staircase – (the beautiful mahogany cupboard was stolen in the 1990s)

The Main Stairwell. Main Stairwell looking East.

The Library in P.Morgan's time – note the beautiful bookcases.

The Library, as a Dining Room when first used as a College.

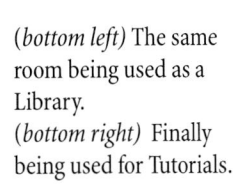

(*bottom left*) The same room being used as a Library.
(*bottom right*) Finally being used for Tutorials.

INTERIOR PHOTOGRAPHS OF THE MANSION 165

The Entrance Hall - looking South.

The Music Room – later, the Staff Common Room.

Photograph from Wall Hall Association Archives.

CHAPTER 18

THE FIFTIETH ANNIVERSARY
1995

THE 50TH ANNIVERSARY – 13 MAY, 1995.

It's my pleasure and privilege to welcome to this 50th Anniversary of Wall Hall as an establishment of education, so many former staff, former students and distinguished guests.

We've been able to build up this event through some fairly extensive advance publicity, since 1945 was of course something of a significant moment in world history, even apart from the foundation of Wall Hall College. Over the last few months we seem to have been virtually re-living the Second World war, in the context of a national celebration for V.E. Day '50 years on.' That celebration, which purported to commemorate a peace, often seemed more focused on the recollection of a war. Memories were drawn back to 1945, it often seemed, as much in nostalgia for the years of war as in mourning over war's loss and destruction. For many of those historical witnesses, listening to them speak, it seemed that 1945 felt like an ending: a moment when a social effort lived in high purpose and inspired by noble values was drawing to a close.

For my generation (I was born in 1947) 1945 certainly represents a beginning. Our cultural formation took place in that period of post-war reconstruction, the world of the welfare State and of the 1944 Education Act. The values of that post-war renaissance - values of community, of public service, of equality of opportunity, of free and universal right to health, social services and education - formed our minds just as surely as the free milk, and the orange juice, and the malt from the big jar in the classroom cupboard, strengthened our brittle little bones.

So I, as an accidental consequence of demobilisation, missed out on the war. I never heard Churchill broadcast; never sang 'Roll out the barrel' in an air-raid shelter; and by the time my teeth had come through, all the G.I's had gone home, taking their bubble-gum (and my Auntie Elizabeth) back to the States with them. But I, (though not enough) of my generation were beneficiaries of the peace, guaranteed access to the education that had been stinted or denied to every previous generation of our people.

The V. E. Day commemoration pointed up just how different was the world of 1945 to that of today; but also found a sense of continuity, the preservation of some abiding values. The Emergency Training College opened at Wall Hall in 1945 became a permanent teacher training College, Wall Hall College; then the School of Education of Hatfield Polytechnic; and is now home to the School of Humanities and Education of the University of Hertfordshire. But all those changes testify to a remarkable continuity: since throughout that half-century Wall Hall has continued to house, in many different ways, the vision and values of education that so strongly motivated that generation which fought and won the peace of 1945.

I'm now delighted to introduce to you a group of children who will exemplify what I've been saying more harmoniously than I could. With some echoes of a world they never knew, and yet which carefully and laboriously were prepared for them, the children of St. John's J.M.I. School, Mill End, will perform with 'Songs from the Evacuees.'

PROFESSOR GRAHAM HOLDERNESS,
Dean of Humanities and Education

(*left*) Past Principals; Staff, Students and Friends gathered together in the Library.

(*right*) The Pupils from St. John's School, Mill End, Rickmansworth, sing their songs.

Wall Hall 50th Anniversary 1995. Ex Principals And Deans.

From left to right:
Dr. Richard Wheeler;
Dr. Derek Haslam;
Miss A. K. Davies;
Professor Graham Holderness.
Sitting: Miss Nancy Dickinson.

WALL HALL ASSOCIATION'S GIFT TO THE DEAN

A typed copy from "The Network" – issue Number 2, July 1995.

The Wall Hall Old Students' Association (Many of whom are also members of the University's Alumni Association) has presented a portrait of the Wall Hall Mansion to Professor Graham Holderness, the Dean of the School of Humanities and Education at Wall Hall. The painting is by a former Art teacher at Wall Hall, Mary Fernandez Morris, and shows the front of the Mansion from across the field. Professor Holderness is pictured with Ann Thorpe, who trained as a teacher at Wall Hall between 1970 and 1973 and currently chairs the Wall Hall Association. The portrait (also pictured) now hangs in the Dean's office.

CHAPTER 19.

OTTERSPOOL

Otter pool milne is referred to in the Aldenham parish records of 1578 and Atterspoole Mill is mentioned in the records of 1638. Otterspoole Milne is listed in The Great Survey as "the mill where all corn has to be ground," according to the Church's ruling.

In the 18th century, that "age of watering places", it was fashionable for the well-to-do to gather at the inland health spas to receive a course of treatment for some ailment, or merely to work off the effects of over indulgence. It is said that such a spa flourished at Otterspool, and indeed, where more convenient for society to enjoy a brief respite from overcrowded 18th century London.

A certificate of recognizance can be seen at the County Record Office showing that John Higgs of Aldenham was licenced to keep a common ale-house or victualling house at Great Otterspool for a term of one year from the 29th day of September 1754.

A newspaper advertisement dated 1766 advertises promises: To be let upon immediately, near Watford, in Hertfordshire. Otterspool Cold Bath with the house, coach-house, brew house, stable. The whole in very good condition being chiefly new built; together with the gardens, orchard and meadows thereto belonging. Enquire of Mr Twyihoe in Essex Court in the Temple or of Thomas Nicholl, attorney at Watford.

It appears that, about the end of the 18th century, Otterspool House became a private residence, for in 1813 the artist Joseph Farington wrote in his diary:

Otterspool – in 1797.

Otterspool – once an 18th century coaching inn on the banks of the River Colne.

September 1813, Friday 3rd.

At 3 o'clock this afternoon I left London in the Watford Coach and went to Otterspool near Watford, the residence of the Hon. Augustus Phipps' servant with a chaise waiting for me and with him I proceeded and got to Otterspool to dinner at ¼ past 6 o'clock. There was not any company and Mr and Mrs. Phipps and myself made a family party.

Mr Phipps told me he had a lease of Otterspool for fifteen years. It was formerly an Inn and celebrated for the powerful springs of water adjoining, a very short distance from the House.

Saturday, 4th September 1813

After breakfast I walked with Mr Phipps to Otterspool Spring near the House. There are two issues of water which together yield 230 gallons of water a minute. The Spring never varies in Summer or Winter. There are two deep holes forming two craters – one 18 feet the other 30 feet deep. Fish not accustomed to this water do not live in it; it is too cold.

Some idea of the appearance of Otterspool at this time can be seen from two prints, one first published in 1797 by J. Sewell, the other published in 1802 by Laurie and Whittle.

A description of the pool was given in the records of the Hertfordshire Natural History Society for 1876 and reads as follows:

Here there is a remarkable pool, at the bottom of which are several gallons of water a day and are said at times some years ago to have yielded a million. These springs are part of a series, which rise along the valley by lowering the reservoir of water in the chalk and here seem mostly due to the rain which falls on the adjoining Eocene area and percolates through the lower Eocene sands and drift gravels into the Chalk. The pool was by sounding, found to be 16 feet deep at the deepest part; and the water is so clear that the springs themselves and the sides of the fissure in the chalk which forms the pool can be distinctly seen and so cold that wine is iced in it.

In that same year, writing on the subject of swallow holes, the same Rev. James Clutterbuck MA, mentions that:

Near Letchmore Heath, in the Parish of Aldenham, where a large body of water sinks in a deep depression or pit into the earth, at the junction of the sand of the Territory beds and the Chalk, this sand may be seen cropping out close at hand.

It has been supposed that there is some connexion between this inflow of water and the well known copious issue at Otterspool. There are stories of ducks having found their way thither by some

(*top left*) Greenhouses and potting sheds, in proposed line of road (1921)
(*top right*) Otterspool Lodge – Spring 2002.
(*bottom left*) View from Otterspool dining room window showing where the proposed (A41) would run – Watford by-Pass.
(*bottom right*) Otterspool Drive – the white mark on the right indicates the central line of the proposed new road (A41) in 1921.

Otterspool House – 1920.

1951 – The Malaysian teachers painting at Otterspool by the Colne

subterranean passage; measurements of the level at which the water stands in the wells thereabout and in the direction of the pool, show an irregularity not easily accounted for but by the existence of some fault or fissure in that direction. After heavy rain the pool becomes slightly turbid and in a dry season it has been known to cease flowing over the dam by which it is confined and over which the water usually falls.

Until the latter half of the 19th century most domestic water supplies came from shallow wells or from the parish pump; then, to combat out-breaks of cholera, typhoid and other water-borne diseases, public water boards were formed and more advanced methods of water supply were developed. The number of epidemics decreased and the amount of water consumed increased.

The growing population, the advances in plumbing, the irrigation of farmland and expanding industry all made further advances on the new public water boards and at Watford and Bushey these demands were met by sinking wells along the Colne Valley Water Company, now part of Three Rivers, and extracting water from the underground sources. Also, in 1794, The grand Junction Canal (later the Grand Union Canal) opened. It took water from the Colne and Otterspool was affected and Tykes Wate. The Aldenham Reservoir was built to top the 56,000 gallon locks. This was also to safeguard the many mills along the river.

The extraction of water may have been this that caused the disappearance of the water at Otterspool, for the falling water level was discussed at a Royal Commission on the Metropolitan Water

Supply in 1893. Mr U. A. Smith said "The mouth of the spring is some 40 feet in diameter and 20 feet deep. The spring yields a much smaller quantity than formerly."

Mr S. T. Holland said: "Since 1873 until 1890 the water had never ceased to run over (the dam that confined the waters, a spit made to form a mill pool.) But in 1890 on several occasions, when with recent lowering of the water table, the sill was perfectly dry and the same occurred again in 1891."

The water level at Otterspool must have continued to drop slowly but surely and the exposed bed was filled with rotting vegetation, later being colonised by plant life to form the water meadows we know today.

In 1798, George Woodford Thellusson leased Otterspool House from a Henry Wood Esq. apparently to provide a home for his daughter and son-in-law the Hon. Mr and Mrs. Augustus Phipps.

When Thellusson died and Wall Hall estate was sold to Sir Charles Morice Pole, his widow, Mary Anne Thellusson, took over Otterspool House. Mary Anne died in 1844, but her daughter remained in residence until 1873. Therafter, Stephen Taprell Holland J.P. occupied the premises until 1923.

After standing vacant for some years, the house became the residence of Captain Jacques Pusinelli. He stayed until 1930 when Henry P. Harland (of Harland and Wolff, the shipbuilders) took up residence.

When Hertfordshire County Council acquired the estate at the end of the Second World War, Otterspool House became a hostel for students of the Wall Hall Teachers' Training College.

Sources: from *Wall Hall in Times Past* "Reflections on a 19th Century Country Estate" Trevor May
The History of Radlett & its Surroundings by Harold Knee.

CHAPTER 20

WALL HALL ASSOCIATION AND THE FIELD GROUP

WALL HALL ASSOCIATION.

Wall Hall College has had a thriving Old Students' Association ever since the early years when the College first opened. It was first called W.H.O.S.A. – Wall Hall Old Students' Association. Some time ago this was modified to W.H.A. – Wall Hall Association. All former of members of Staff and Students can become members, with friends of the Association being voted to join too, paying a nominal membership fee.

The Association holds a Reunion and Annual General Meeting once a year and the Committee members meet at least once, sometimes twice a year.

Every year too, members who have paid their subscription monies, receive a Newsletter. Members who have any news, send this to be edited and published, which makes very interesting reading, especially for those people who are unable to travel to the Re-Union, either because of the journeys involved; for holidays; or health or age reasons. It has been an extremely useful contact between all past Staff and Students, helping to keep in touch with each other and various Year Groups formed whilst we were training

The Field Group Association in 1994.

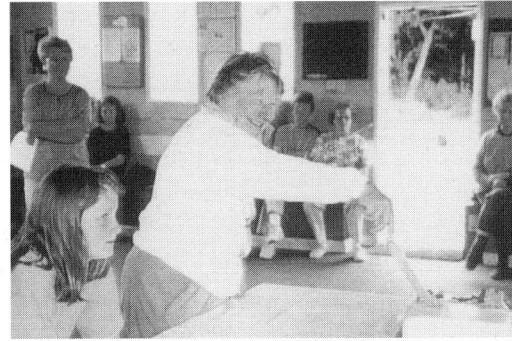

Wall Hall Reunion 1993

(*top right*) Miss Kay Davies talking to Miss Nancy Dickinson

Members exchanging views

to be teachers. These Newsletters have been invaluable in us being able to extract photographs, letters and items, which have been used in the compilation of the book you are now holding.

The Chairman has written a letter annually to all of the current members on the mailing list, (which has been another way of "keeping in touch" and for information.) In the new year it has been the custom for the secretary to notify everyone of the forthcoming A.G.M. and Reunion date and arrangements for the after dinner Speaker. These have been extremely interesting and very varied in their content – there have also been several recitals of

176 WALL HALL FROM FARMHOUSE TO UNIVERSITY

Wall hall Assocation –
AGM and Reunion 2001

Photos by Joan Beagle

Wall Hall reunion 2001 – lunch in Refectory

Reunion 2002
Afternoon tea

Last chats and goodbyes

(*top*) Lake District 1957?
– led by Margaret Smeaton
(*top right*) Stoke-on-Trent1980s
(*centre*) Abingdon outing 1989
(*bottom*) Yorkshire Dales 1995

music and hand bell ringing! There is a also 'sister' Association called The Field Group Association. Quite a few W.H.A. members belong to this group too.

THE FIELD GROUP

This body first met in 1964 when Joan Stampe, Margaret Smeaton and a handful of ex-students visited the Experimental Research

Field Week Trip to Morewellham Quay (Devon Week) 1980's.

Field Group – London Walk outing 2001

Station at Rothamstead. Initially the visits were of a biological or geographical nature, but it soon became obvious that anything educational would be both enjoyable and would furnish ideas for the classroom. In addition to days out, weekends and whole weeks have been spent in the pursuit of education and fun. There are about six visits a year with an Annual General Meeting in the winter and the exploits are many and varied: from Bell Foundry to Botany, old musical instruments to burial mounds, glaciers and graveyards, town walks to conservation schemes, old schools to new roads; wherever the venue, the richness of the environment and heritage is enjoyed together with the informal company of friends and family.

Margaret Smeaton (former Geography Tutor.)

The visits organised can sometimes be near Wall Hall, or in London, or, in summertime, further afield to areas in Devon, Hampshire, Sussex, Essex, Norfolk or Yorkshire. This means members living a long way away usually have at least one meeting a year within a reasonable distance to them.

Because of the move by the Campus of Wall Hall to the University of Hertfordshire Hatfield Campus in 2003, the Wall Hall Association will cease to exist, but the Field Group will continue to function. All members of Wall Hall College (College of Education) can become a member of the University's Alumni Association – they would be able to organise their own year group re-union, should they wish to do this, through the Alumni Association – Reunions @ herts.ac.uk

CHAPTER 21

THE PARISH CHURCH AT ALDENHAM

Permission to print the text from "A Brief Guide" to the Church and to take photographs of the windows and memorial brasses has been given by the Vicar of the Parish Church, Robert Fletcher.

PARISH CHURCH OF ST. JOHN THE BAPTIST, ALDENHAM

A chapter dedicated to this Church is included because Wall Hall Manor owners worshipped there or had Brasses or Inscriptions dedicated to them by their families and when Wall Hall College was established, there have been close links with it. Dedication Day and End of Term services were always held there. The Principals, Tutors, Students and visiting Dignitaries played integral roles in the services. Up to the present day, the church is still used by students for their course work in Religious Education and History.

The earliest document mentioning the village of Aldenham is dated 785 A.D. In it King Offa of Mercia gives lands in Aldenham to

St. John the Baptist Church, Aldenham.

Aldenham Church - showing the Nave.

King Offa holding a Saxon Church (East window)

The window depicting Edward the Confessor – replaced after being destroyed by the 1939–1945 war-time bomb damage.

Photographs by Pat Saunders (née Insall.)

the Abbot of Westminster in exchange for a gold amulet. Offa appears in the East Window holding a Saxon church.

The settlement of Aldenham is mentioned in the Domesday Survey of 1086. It was an agricultural community and there are references to a mill, nine hides (a hide was a measure of land about 120 acres) owned by the Abbot of Westminster and one hide of land for the plough held by Geoffrey of Be, "but the plough is missing." There is good reason to believe that a Saxon church stood on the present site, although the oldest parts of the present Church is much more recent than that. Records show that there was a Vicar of the Parish as early as 1267; his name was Roger and records indicate him purchasing a house which stood between the Church and Otterspool for which he paid Geoffrey of Walehale, ten shillings. (Might this have been Wall Hall?)

Around 1250, there was a complete rebuild of the Church and substantial portions of this building can still be found. The 14th. Century saw the building of the South aisle (*c.*1340) followed some hundred years later by the North aisle (*c.*1450) and only a short time after that, by a splendid painted oak ceiling in the Nave.

The Stepney Arms can be found on the Stepney tomb at the West end of the knave in front of the baptistry. All that remains is a shield on the top right hand side of the tomb – half of another shield (top left) is in the safe in the vestry.

> The inscription reads:
>
> > Here lyeth Stepney Esquyre, the first Lord of the Lordship of this Towne of Aldenham, and Patron of this Church, who dyed 3. Decmb. 1544 on whos sowl Iusa have mercy. Amen"
>
> This date of 1544 as quoted by Weever and Chauncey, is obviously incorrect as he only inherited the Manor in 1547 and therefore must have been alive to receive it!
>
> In the Vestry wall safe are 2 Palimpsest brasses – these are Brasses which have been laid down a second time on the opposite side to that used originally and subsequently re-engraved with a new inscription or figure.
>
> The first Brass is part of the Coat of Arms granted to Ralph Stepney. The figure appears to have been a man in armour; the shields are:
>
> > (Colour) a fesse chaque (metal and colour, or and azure respectively) between three owls (metal, argent) impaling quarterly of 4: 1 and 1V (illegible) 11 and 111 argent, 3 bars (colour)
> > The man's Arms are those of Stepney:
> > Gules, a fesse chaque (or and azure,) between 3 owls (argent.)
> > His Arms are quartered with those of his wife, Joan Cressy.
> > Arms: (argent) a lion rampant (sable)
>
> The engraver who incised this shield made a mistake. The Fesse in Stepney's Arms should have been Compony and not Chaque.

The Stepney Arms

The Carey family were well known in court circles and Sir Edward Carey was a groom of the Privy Chamber at the court of Elizabeth the first. He was knighted in 1596. He had nine children, six daughters and three sons. All the eldest daughters except Elizabeth (the eldest) married Knights and his eldest son Henry was created Viscount Falkland and Lord Carey 1620. Although parish records attest that many of the family of Carey were buried at Aldenham, only one memorial remains and that is to a daughter of Sir Edward Carey who was married to Sir Thomas Crompton. This memorial is to Meriall, third daughter of Sir Edward Carey and the tablet can be seen on the South wall of the chancel, just below where her father's helmet was once placed. This was stolen, but recovered and is now held in the bank.

A print of the Church dated 1768 looks remarkably similar to the building today. Inside however, several large restoration and alterations went on during the next century and a half. In 1813, a survey declared parts of the building in a "state of Dilapidation and Decay" and the following year, the spire was found to be (*left*) Aldenham Church after the 16th. August 1940 (no spire.)

(*right*) Aldenham Church with its spire returned – repairs began in 1946.
Photographs from Josie Weatherley

Memorial Window in the South Aisle marks the 50th. Anniversary to the sinking of H.M.S. Aldenham, a hunt class destroyer, sunk by a mine in the Adriatic sea in 1944, with a loss of 116 men.
Photograph by Pat Saunders.

dangerously decayed. The 50 cwts. of lead with which it was clad might well have caused it to topple through the Tower, carrying the Belfry with it. The architect, a Mr John Shaw, described Aldenham as "one of the most beautiful village churches I have ever seen."

After George W. Thellusson's death in 1812, the manor passed to his nephew John Thellusson who became the 19th. Lord of the Manor of Aldenham. John held the Manor until his death in 1832, when it passed to his uncle, William Thellusson – becoming the 20th Lord of the Manor. (William had become Vicar of Aldenham in 1825 which position he held until 1833.) Thellusson manuscripts which are held at Suffolk Record Office in Ipswich states "As there is no Manor House in which to live, the Thellussons lived in Wall Hall, which originally was "no more than a modest farmstead."

In 1843, using £300 borrowed by the Churchwardens, more work was done including the removal of the musicians' gallery from under the Tower and, in 1847, the Chancel was renovated and the present waggon-headed roof was replaced the lower flat, whitewashed ceilings. The most significant alterations were carried out in 1882 by Henry Huck Gibbs (later Lord Aldenham) at a cost of £11,000 and during these, the Rood Loft and the Priests' door with its adjoining window were discovered. The present Altar, Credence table. Pulpit and Lectern were all donated by Henry Huck Gibbs at this time and also a new organ which cost £721 to build.

The village surrounding the church owes its present appearance, to the planning and patronage of American banker John Pierpont Morgan, whom after acquiring Wall Hall built the semi-circle of white cottages on the green and others like it in the village, for his estate workers and turned neighbouring Church Farm (now renamed Manor House) into an efficiently managed model farm.

The final phase in the evolution of the building was the direct result of enemy action. On 16 October 1940, a stray stick of bombs fell around the churchyard, demolishing the Spire which, in falling, caused damage to the Tower and Nave roof. Several windows were lost including the Great East Window. Repair of the damage began in 1946 and included the redesign of the Spire and the Chancel, complete electrical rewiring and a new East Window. After the war, of the renovation's total of £9,500, £3,500 was raised by Parishioners and a Thanksgiving service was held in September 1951 at which the new East Window was dedicated. It contains some poignant memories of the war as well as many other references to the church's past.

Naval wartime connections are also evident. The first grave on the left outside the North door has an inscription to Robert Smith, a Midshipman on H.M.S. Victory, killed at Trafalgar. The tattered white ensign near the chancel arch is from H.M.S. Aldenham, a hunt class destroyer sunk by a mine in the Adriatic Sea in 1944 with the loss of 116 men. A memorial window in the South aisle marks the 50th anniversary of the sinking and a memorial service is held each year.

Since then, fresh outbreaks of death watch beetle have been combatted, the roof repaired, the Tower strengthened and all the usual maintenance problems solved by local contributions and, the building today is as healthy as an enthusiastic and loyal community can keep it.

One of the Vicars of Aldenham Parish Church the Reverend Henry Huck Gibbs, later Lord Aldenham (standing on the left of picture.) He made the most significant changes to the Church in 1882 at a cost of £11,000. The present altar, credence table, pulpit, lectern were all donated by him and new a organ which cost £721 to build.

This text has been taken from *The Guide to the Parish Church of St. John the Baptist Church* by John Meloy and David Robertson

CHAPTER 22

COUNTRY WALKS AROUND WALL HALL

Information from various sources indicates there were early roads and tracks nearby and crossing the Wall Hall Estate. To the east is Watling Street which was an old British track that was used and developed by the Romans and eventually ran from near Sandwich in Kent to Chaster. North of London (Londinium) it is now called the Edgware Road. After running past Edgware it passes over Brockley Hill, where remains of Roman pottery kilns have been found and into Elstree where it is again called Watling Street. It continues to St. Albans (Verulamium) then northwards round Birmingham and north-west to Chester.

There is some evidence to suggest Watling Street divided at Elstree and a side branch followed roughly the line of the present Aldenham Road, past Haberdasher Aske's School and Aldenham School. Roman tiles have been found in the grounds of both schools. It then crossed what used to be the Great Common of Aldenham and across Common Lane to Battlers Green. Here it met a track that ran down to Watling Street as it went through the area of Radlett. This track was probably the present Loom Lane, where again Roman pottery has been found with CASTUS the potter's name etched on them.

At Battlers Green the minor road divided – one branch went across the fields, skirting the site of the Moated Homestead, to High Cross, Kemprow, Blackbirds Lane and down towards the River Colne and Munden. The other branch (which may have been called Ingold Street) went south-west towards Delrow, then northwards towards

The road leading to the River Colne and then joining Crab Lane.

Aldenham Church, the north-west across the Wall Hall Estate. It followed the same route as the old coach road.

It went towards the River Colne and joined Common Meadow Lane. Crab Lane is part of a pre-historic track that ran between Radlett and Watford, which became the drive to Wall Hall. As well as the remains of Roman a Villa at Munden, tiles and pots have been found. Many of these can be seen in the Verulamium Museum at St. Albans.It skirted the edge of the wetlands (which had resulted from the ice-melt of the Anglian Ice Age,) then joined Blackbird Lane and Common Meadow Lane (so called because this is where the Common Fields were situated in feudal times, the alluvial soil of the old flood plain providing rich pasture.)

After crossing the River Colne by a ford north of Munden, the combined road went through Brickett Wood to Valence End Road Farm at Eaton Way near Whipsnade, where it joined the Icknield Way.

When the Romans left, some of these roads fell into disuse and had to be cleared years later. Parts of some were included in fields and became overgrown. Gradually other roads were made, at first for horse travel and drovers and then for coaches. A few roads were closed or re-routed. The Enclosure Act of 1801 closed some of them and new roads were built to replace them. Today some which were closed survive as Bridle Ways or Public Footpaths.

One footpath runs along the drive and passes Wall Hall Mansion and then down to the old road to the River Colne. This may be followed as part of the Ver-Colne Valley Walk, towards St. Albans and Redbourn. En route several old watermills will be passed, built mainly to grind corn in the Middle Ages, when grinding by hand was forbidden by the Church. Many have been converted for

(*top*) The River Colne and footbridge (a footpath sign is at the end of it)

(*below*) The floodplain under water in 2002

different usages – some into a Museum with restaurant, examples being Kingsbury Mill at St. Albans, Redbournbury Mill and Moor Mill near Munden.

After turning southwards from Wall Hall the Linear Walk is joined which goes through Watford following the River Colne, then joins the Grand Union Canal/ Colne Valley Walk, to Rickmansworth,Denham and Uxbridge.

Lakes made from gravel workings are passed on the way to the Thames Valley. The railway roughly follows this route from Redbourn to the Thames, so it is possible to make a train ride back to where your car is parked! The flood plain near Wall Hall still gets extensively flooded after heavy rain, as clearly portrayed in the photograph below, taken in the early months of 2002.

The River Colne still runs freely here, although a few side streams have dried up, including the old lily pond. The footbridge now spans a wide expanse of rushes. In its upper reaches the River Ver has dried up north of Redbournbury. It is thought to be due to the ever larger supplies of water being pumped via boreholes from deep within the chalk, to supply the increasing population in the area. (Something which should be considered when even more housing expansion is planned.) Otterspool, once 22 feet deep, sadly is no longer that depth, but is still fed for the time being, by several of its springs.

Wall Hall Estate includes the Berrygrove Woods and the Aldenham Golf Club course, rented farms, woodlands and other properties. There is a pleasant and interesting walk through Berrygrove Woods, which is a managed woodland, in agreement with the Forestry Commission. The actual work is carried out by the Hertfordshire County Council Land Agents forestry staff, based at Wall Hall, who maintain woods throughout the County. It is a fascinating example of a modern working wood. These woods were once managed by John Pierpont Morgan Jnr. the last private owner of Wall Hall, for his sporting interests. They were far more extensive then, but land was taken from them for the construction of the A41 Watford By-Pass in the 1930's and then in 1962 for the M1. – originally the M1 started at Berrygrove before it was later extended to the North Circular Road. These woods show how commercial timber harvesting can be successfully combined with conservation and recreation.

The walk starts near Aldenham Village and goes through and

round the woods to return round the edge of the Golf Course and the drive to Wall Hall, thence back to Aldenham Village. There are other footpaths radiating out from Aldenham Village, some probably walked by the villagers to attend services at Aldenham Church. These go to Blackbirds Farm, Round Bush, Battlers Green, Letchmore Heath, Aldenham School, Haberdasher Aske's School, Elstree Village, Elstree Aerodrome and Aldenham Country Park. All of these places were once within the Great Common of Aldenham, which stretched southwards beyond Aldenham Reservoir.

So members of the Wall Hall Association, staff, old colleagues and friends, should still be able to look across to the River Colne valley, walk through the grounds of Wall Hall and gaze again at the cedar trees and daffodils, which are expected to be preserved.

Pictorial maps of walks in the area, which can also be easily walked by children, may be obtained from:
The Country Management Service, Blanche Farm, Blanche Lane,
   Potters Bar, Herts. EN6 3LF.
These include: Berrygrove Woods – a working woodland trail.
The Roundbush Ramble.
The Three Hamlet Ramble.

Other sources: The Hertfordshire Way – a walker's guide book, edited
   by Bert Richardson.
The Bricket Wood Society.
The Ramblers Society.
The Footpaths Society.
Ordnance Survey Maps, including O.S. Pathfinder Map no: 1139,
   Watford and Rickmansworth.
William Page – *A History of the Manor of Wall Hall in Hertfordshire.*
Harold J. Knee – *History of Radlett and its Surroundings.*
Verulamium Museum.
Material held in Hertfordshire County Archives – including maps.

CHAPTER 23

CONCLUSION

Owners of the Manor of Wall Hall, since it came into existence some eight centuries ago, have played a distinguished part in the history of our country. They have represented every walk of life. Merchants and financiers like Saer, son of Henry; Sir Job Harby; Samuel Vandewall; George Woodford Thellusson; Thomas Neate and John Pierpont Morgan Jnr. Ecclesiastics such as the great Chancellor Burnell and the Priors of St. Bartholomew. A sailor as Morice Pole. Soldiers like Sir Richard Somery. Politicians such as The Careys, Denzil Holles and Duke of Newcastle. Civil servants such as Adam de Stratton and Richard de Eccleshale.

Pierpont Morgan also had already been pasteurising milk, well before it was deemed necessary for the installation of plant to enable this process to be carried out nationwide. Each one of these prominent men played his part in the events which gradually developed the nation and also the world as we find them today.

Since Wall Hall became a College of Education, this tradition has been continued, with countless numbers of student teachers receiving the best of educational practice from dedicated tutors. These teachers went on to give their pupils not only a basis for living in the community, but the academic tools to enrich and further their own potential aspirations. Miss Nancy Dickinson, whilst working in the Divisional Education Office (before being offered the position of being the second Principal at Wall Hall) reorganised the basis for Secondary Education in Hertfordshire and helped to draw up development plans for many new schools. She encouraged mature students to enter the field of teaching. Wall Hall was in the forefront of catering for the Teaching of mentally handicapped and deaf impaired children, training many men and women in this specialised field of work.

Innumerable young and mature people have, over the past sixty years, had the privilege of learning how to teach and acquire new skills at Wall Hall. They have been encouraged by Principals and Lecturers to pass on their knowledge to many numbers of young children and at the same time to continue to widen their own horizons. They have, whilst living in all areas of the British Isles and in many other countries of the World, taught children of every colour and different religious beliefs. To have had the opportunity, whilst in the process of being trained to be teachers, to study in and around the resplendent Mansion and being able to pursue knowledge at Wall Hall College, set in the beautiful, tranquil gardens and grounds, designed by Humphrey Repton, is something all who studied and worked there will never forget. They treasure many happy memories of their colleagues and Tutors made whilst in the process of learning. They will miss too, the yearly visits back to Wall Hall, when it will no longer be possible after 8, to have the opportunity to gather there to meet friends and colleagues at the Wall Hall Old Students' Annual Reunions.

So will end after many centuries, yet another episode in the colourful history of a simple dwelling place, which began as a lowly Farmhouse becoming transformed into a University. The next chapter in its long history will see a new era for its function, with the possibility of the Estate being renewed to some of its former splendours with the intended development of luxury apartments and houses.

DAPHNE TILLEY.

SOURCES.

A History of the Manor of Wall Hall in Hertfordshire, William Page 1920
    Unpublished document.
A. K. Davies – Former Principal
Book of Radlett and Aldenham, Donald Wratton.
Collection on some Aspects of the History of Radlett and its Surroundings,
    H. J. Knee, 1974
Dr. Paul Williamson – Victoria and Albert Museum
E. Greenall, Former Librarian at Wall Hall.
Guide to the Parish Church of St. John the Baptist, John Meloy and David
    Robertson (1990).
Hertfordshire Archives and Local Studies (HALS).
    (a) Postcard – St. Alban's Abbey.
    Postcard – Monks in Procession.
    (b) Texts from History of Hertfordshire Vol:2, 1908.

(c) John, Duke of Newcastle and Clare.
(d) 1766 map by Andrew Dury & John Andrews.
(e) Poster, sale of Wall Hall Estate 1812.
(f) Map of Wall Hall Estate 1812. (D/P3/29/2B).
(g) Press cuttings of 10th Anniversary.
(h) Foundation Day – 20th Anniversary, texts & photographs. (OFF ACC 700 Box 4)
(i) Courses at Wall Hall, 1975.

Hertfordshire University Alumni Paper "The Network" July 1995.
Hertfordshire University – "Our Heritage" by Tony Gardner.
H. Kernohan – photograph.
Joan Beagle – photographs
K. J. Ming – A former part-time student at Wall Hall
Mary Hood
Margaret Smeaton – Former Geography Lecturer at Wall Hall.
Norman Thomas, CBE – An address given to Staff and Students 1995.
Pat Saunders
Photographs from past and present Principals, Lecturers, Administrative & Domestic Staff and former Students of Wall Hall
Photographs from various Prospectus books from Wall Hall
Professor Chris Cook – Interior photographs
The History of the Manor of Aldenham in Hertfordshire – David Robertson, 1993.
The West Herts. and Watford Advertiser, 1945
The Pierpont Morgan Library, New York
Trevor May, Former History Lecturer at Wall Hall
Newsletters of the Old Students' Association
Vicar of Aldenham Church – Robert Fletcher
Verulamium and St. Albans Museums
Wall Hall Association Archives
Wall Hall in Times Past – Trevor May's tutorial group, 1981